The Last Chapter

D1468736

The Last Chapter

Gene Amole on Dying

Gene Amole

Rocky Mountain News
DENVER

Johnson Books
BOULDER

Published by Johnson Books, a division of Johnson Publishing Company, 1880 South 57th Court, Boulder, Colorado 80301. E-mail: books@jpcolorado.com.

9 8 7 6 5 4 3 2

Cover design by Debra B. Topping
Cover photo: Gene Amole, with daughter Tustin and son Jonathan, leaves the *Rocky Mountain News* for the last time after a ceremony renaming Elati Street as Gene Amole Way on Dec. 20, 2001. (photo by Ellen Jaskol, *Rocky Mountain News*)

Library of Congress Cataloging-in-Publication Data
Amole, Gene, 1923–
   The last chapter: Gene Amole on dying / Gene Amole.
   p. cm.
   ISBN 1-55566-282-X
   1. Amole, Gene, 1923–   —Death and burial. 2. Journalists
—United States—Biography. I. Title.
   PN4874.A46A3 2002
   070´.92-dc21
   [B]

2002008556

Printed in the United States by
Johnson Printing
1880 South 57th Court
Boulder, Colorado 80301

 Printed on recycled paper with soy ink

Contents

Farewell, friend; your voice lives on

(From the publisher of the *Rocky Mountain News*)

The *Rocky Mountain News* is proud to republish a selection of Gene Amole's Diary of Dying. Gene stunned his readers with a column on October 27, 2001, announcing that he had decided to stop fighting all the ailments that were plaguing him. He died on May 12, 2002. In between, lifted by the loving response of his readers, family and colleagues, he wrote feverishly. During one 17-week stretch, the *News* published a column by Gene every day it published. It was a remarkable experience for the newspaper and the city. It was a final gift from a native son who loved his hometown and the people who live here. The profits from this book will go to the Hospice of Metro Denver, which cared for Gene in his final months. The book itself is dedicated to his wife, Trish, and family, whose love he appreciated above all else.

The following is an excerpt of a column I wrote to Gene the day he died. It remains how I feel today.

FRIEND.

This is the only day I will borrow your trademark of a single opening word.

I promise you. Because if you have taught me anything, you have taught me the power of a person true to himself.

We talked often of death. Your most powerful writing was of World War II, of the friends you lost. You always told me that they did not *give* their lives. That their lives were *taken* from them.

Somehow it seemed you knew that your survival meant you owed it to them to live your life to the fullest.

We were all the better for it.

You taught us to live the same way. Your spirit made this a better place to live and work.

You were the heart of the *Rocky.* Time passed, people changed, but there you always were with your love of the town and your belief in telling it like it is.

We all knew your simple refrain: Write to express, not to impress.

And we all tried to take it to heart. It seemed so easy for you. But I knew how hard you worked to make it read that way.

We often talked of how you never wanted to stop. Even in our last conversation, when you had just arrived home from the hospital, you told me you had much to say, much that you wanted to write.

When you slipped away, Stan Getz was playing in the background. I don't know if you heard him or not. But it's only fitting that you would leave us to the sound of jazz.

You brought music to the hearts of so many. You lifted their lives with your voice and the music you played over the airwaves to start their day.

It was astonishing to see the reaction after you told your readers that you were dying. So many strangers wrote you about how you were their friend. You had the rare ability to touch people with your voice, with your words.

You were comfortable in yourself, in your views. They knew that you were the real thing.

Now you've danced your last waltz.

But we will still celebrate your sounds, the words that connected us.

We will miss you, friend. I know you had more to say. Now I will have to imagine your voice.

I can hear it now. It is strong. It is rich.

It is Denver.

John Temple
Editor, president and publisher
Rocky Mountain News

Forever young:
"Voice of Denver" Gene Amole dies at 78

(Obituary from the *Rocky Mountain News*)

DENVER HAS LOST A GIANT.

Gene Amole, a newspaper columnist who celebrated the city he loved and fought those who would change it forever, died Sunday, 12 days shy of his 79th birthday.

Amole, who had been in declining health for several years, died at his home of multi-systems failure.

Gene was best known for his columns in the *Rocky Mountain News*, but it was a role he didn't come to until he was 54.

Long before then, he was a broadcasting pioneer, popular radio and television personality, shrewd businessman, war correspondent and GI in the killing fields of Hitler's Europe.

"Gene Amole was the voice of this city and the heart of this newspaper," News Editor and Publisher John Temple said. "He always called himself an ordinary guy. In fact, he was an extraordinary person because he could communicate in such a direct and genuine way."

Gene announced to his readers on Oct. 27 that he was dying. But he said he intended to continue to write a diary of his experiences that he hoped would help others. And indeed he did.

With characteristic clarity, he wrote of the insight that came with deepening physical infirmity, of treasuring the richness of waning days. His craftsmanship with the written word did not betray him. His humor, his compassion, his celebration of this place, his love for friends and most particularly his family came shining through.

"I truly believe I'm the most lucky dying man still alive," he wrote.

Writing his "diary pages" seemed to give him new vigor. In one incredible stretch, Gene wrote in every edition of the *News*—six days per week—for 17 consecutive weeks.

During that time, he realized a dream by returning to Hawaii with most of his family, including his beloved grandson, Jacob. From there, he wrote of "watching morning rainbows bridge across Lahaina Bay" and seeing "tropical birds roller-coaster on cool trade-wind gusts."

He wished his readers could see it with him, he wrote.

His readers responded throughout with an outpouring of love and support, in e-mails and letters.

In December, Mayor Wellington Webb announced the city was renaming a street for Gene. Appropriately, that stretch of Elati Street that borders the *Rocky Mountain News* became Gene Amole Way.

"This community is a better place because of Gene," Webb said. "Denver has lost a living legend, a modern-day pioneer and a great human being."

Gene Amole was a son, a husband, a father and, finally, to his bubbling delight at the age of 72, a grandfather.

For nearly 25 years, his prose chronicled Denver's leap from an insular midsized city into a throbbing high-tech capital of the New West.

With a blend of bluntness, whimsy and vivid detail, Gene made it clear he didn't like those who would forever change the face of Denver.

He savaged civic leaders he believed were fleecing citizens or turning the Denver he fiercely loved into a megalopolis distinct from nowhere else.

Three times a week, he was Denver's conscience, scold and cheerleader—but most of all its chief purveyor of straight talk.

He was an implacable foe of the construction of Denver International Airport, unbridled growth and taxpayer subsidies for big business.

"It still bothers me that we are paying for a baseball field but don't get to name it," he wrote in 1995 after Coors Field opened to rave reviews by baseball fans and downtown business owners. "Instead of Taxpayers Field, which should have been its name, it is Coors Field because the Coors brewery has more clout than you and I do."

But Gene tried hard not to be a nag. A soft streak as warm as melted butter smoothed the rough edges of his most pointed writing.

He regularly summoned images of Denver's history and beauty—the old neighborhoods where he grew up, the inviting crispness of an October morning.

His Colorado roots ran deep. His mother's father was a farmer in Ohio when a brother contracted tuberculosis, and the family moved to Colorado for the dry air. His father's father, "Grandpa Amole," ran away from home in Ohio when he was 15 and made his way to Denver. It was 1877.

A sturdy house in north Denver was home to five generations of Amoles. It was built by Gene's great-grandfather, Will Fiedler, at the turn of the century.

"It's a comfortable old place with an ancient apple tree in the back yard," Gene wrote in 1993. "On snowy, cold days when the steam radiators are clanking, something magic happens. There is the faint but unmistakable aroma of chicken and dumplings coming out of the kitchen, and sometimes I think I can actually see Grandma Lizzie standing there beside the stove."

Colorado historian Tom Noel said he "clipped" Gene's columns for years to use in lectures, tours, articles, columns and books.

"He had a marvelous ability to recall the past in vivid detail that made you see, hear, smell and even taste Colorado history. He was a courageous, eloquent voice."

Gene was the voice of old Denver, an unabashed nostalgic who regularly recalled the sights, scents and sounds of an earlier, simpler time on the flanks of the Rocky Mountains.

He wrote about Pop, Grandpa, Grandma, home-baked pies and autumn's leaves, often mingling images of life's joys and drudgeries in the same column. About attending meetings as he neared 60, Gene wrote:

"The minute someone stands up and says, 'I think it is important for us to establish meaningful guidelines,' the mind begins to slip away.

"My thoughts sometimes wander to fresh baked apple pie. I can just see the brown, syrupy Jonathan apple juice bubble up through the slits on the top crust. I silently wonder if there is any Swiss cheese in the refrigerator."

In 1995, he described the joys of October:

"I love tiny bedsheet ghosts at my door, pot roast simmering in the kitchen, slipping into a favorite old sweater, the moon close enough to touch, that first cup of hot cocoa, cattails and pussy willows in the marsh, lopsided pumpkin faces, crayon witches and goblins on refrigerator doors."

Nowhere was his underlying optimism about life more visible than in his first column for the *News*, published December 18, 1977. It led off with the first of what would become his trademark—a pithy word or phrase to kick-start his tales.

"Morning," Gene began simply.

"It is the innocent time of day. The air is clean. A small black dog frisks through a familiar backyard routine. The light is bright from the window of an East Colfax all-night coffee shop. Great flights of Canada geese rise swiftly from suburban reservoirs.

"Downtown, the first trash and delivery trucks clank through half-empty streets. Street lights and neon signs go out as the new day's light begins to fill the sky.

"There is the aroma of fresh coffee. It makes its secret way out of the kitchen and up the stairs. Soapy water swirls into the drain, and the clean, white terry cloth towel brings life to a body not quite ready for the day."

His *News* columns were compiled in three volumes, including, most recently, *Amole One More Time.*

Frank Eugene Amole Jr. was born an only child in northwest Denver on May 24, 1923. He was a third-generation Coloradan.

As a boy, his life's ambition was to be a soldier. He would soon get his wish.

Gene graduated in 1941 from South High School. He enrolled at the University of Colorado but quickly found college boring and flunked out. He was pulling down $75 a week as a bellhop at the old Cosmopolitan Hotel when broadcasting beckoned.

After being turned down by every radio station in town several times, he finally got a job as a clerk with KMYR radio at 1626 Stout St. Gene became, in his words, the station's "traffic girl." His starting salary: $22 a week.

Before long, he got a shot at announcing, largely on the strength of his portrayal of Harold Ickes, Franklin Roosevelt's interior secretary, on a KOA radio drama.

But World War II was on, and he was soon drafted by the Army. On February 10, 1944, he and the rest of the 6th Armored Division embarked from Pier 89 in New York to join General George Patton's sweep across Europe.

Even a half-century after his harrowing duty in the Battle of the Bulge and other campaigns, it was clear that the war was Gene Amole's defining moment.

As the 50th anniversary of the end of the war approached in 1995, Gene wrote:

"Forever young.

"What do you say to a high school girl who calls on the phone and wants to know what it is like to kill someone? What do you think about, she wondered, when you look down at the body? Do you feel guilt?

"That happened to me the other day when she called for help in writing a report for a history class on World War II. She wanted to know what we had to eat, where we learned how to make war and how we felt about what we did.

"It's no use trying to get the war out of your system. Just when you think its horror and ugliness have slipped beyond recall, something comes up to make it live again.

"I will probably never get over the anguish I still feel for the dead. And those of us who managed to survive still are haunted with the guilt of living while others died. We will always ask ourselves the question, 'Why them and not us?' They did not give their lives. Their lives were taken from them.

"My way of coping with these troubling thoughts 50 years later is not to remember them as forever dead, but as forever young."

After the war, Gene returned to Denver and rejoined KMYR. There, he met Ed Koepke, who became a close friend and longtime broadcast business partner.

They founded AM jazz radio station KDEN in 1956 and launched KVOD, an FM station, a year later.

Gene took his broadcasting talent to the street. He interviewed an estimated 10,000 people, in daily man-on-the-street programs at 16th Street and Glenarm Place and in chats with celebrities including Dwight Eisenhower, James Stewart, Robert Mitchum, Otto Preminger and Douglas MacArthur.

KVOD, "the classical voice of Denver," became one of the nation's most successful classical music stations, and it made Gene a reluctant broadcasting star.

Gene was a radio rarity—a station co-owner who spent hours every day on the air. A gifted programmer, he filled the prime 6–10 a.m. slot, and he knew what kind of music to play. Listeners and advertisers couldn't get enough of him.

"I've found that when people awaken in the morning, they want to hear something familiar," he said in 1979. "They don't want to deal with something unknown, and the music has to be 'up' because they don't want something draggy. And they don't want to hear something long because they won't have time to hear the end of it. Short, bright, familiar, and not always orchestral—maybe a guitar, a piano."

His listeners didn't appreciate the need for commercials.

"You may not like that commercial, but that commercial made it possible for you to hear Beethoven's Ninth Symphony," Gene once explained.

Gene and partner Koepke, however, drew a line. They would not play commercials between the movements of a symphony.

Even competitors in the bruising fight for audience share praised Gene.

"He's the last, great, eternally appealing radio personality in this city," Steve Keeney, general manger of KIMN and KYGO-FM, said of Gene in 1979. "His radio station may be the finest classical music station in the country."

As he demonstrated later at the *News*, Gene was much more than a radio personality. He spent seven months as a war correspondent during the Korean War, filing dispatches for *The Denver Post* and the Mutual Broadcasting System. He reported from behind the Iron Curtain during the Berlin blockade of 1948, and also wrote about the new nation of Israel.

When the age of television dawned, Gene immediately was a writer and producer, then a sportscaster, weatherman and news anchor. He was doing live commercials on Channel 2 the first week Denver had regular TV programming in 1952. He also worked for Channels 4, 6, 7 and 9.

Panorama, a live, weekly public affairs program he wrote and narrated, won a George Foster Peabody award—broadcast journalism's highest honor, in 1957. He won an Emmy for a television portrait of poet Thomas Hornsby Ferril. Gene also did one of TV's first talk programs.

Perhaps his biggest television coup was his exclusive jailhouse interview of John Gilbert Graham, convicted of blowing up a United Airlines passenger plane in 1955 and killing 44 people. Graham, who placed dynamite in his mother's suitcase and hoped to collect her flight insurance, was later executed.

Graham's sensational trial was broadcast on the radio station owned by Gene and Koepke. Gene and *News* photographer Morey Engle sneaked camera equipment into the old Denver County Jail for the Graham interview. But no Denver TV station would carry the footage, fearing it might engender sympathy for Graham before his trial.

It was finally shown, four decades later in 1995, on Colorado public television station KRMA-Channel 6.

Gene retired from broadcasting in 1983 when he and Koepke sold KVOD for a reported $6.4 million.

When he started at the *News* in 1977, Gene really didn't need the money or the job. But he kept at it, through bouts of ill health, long after many others would have retired.

There was no fancy corner office for Gene. A newsman above all else, he insisted on a desk barely 10 feet from the city desk, the newsroom's nerve center. He thrived on the controlled chaos swirling around him every day.

"Honestly, I am so pleased to be here," he told readers in his inaugural column. "To be a writer for the *News* has been my longtime, not-so-secret ambition."

It was a sentiment he cherished the rest of his life.

His only fear, he often said, was overstaying his welcome. In a 1988 column, Gene, just turned 65, said he had no plans to retire. But he added:

"I just hope I have the good sense to know when it is time to leave gracefully. So many old fools stay too long at the fair.

"… Let's make a deal. When it becomes obvious that I am losing it, have the decency to take me aside and whisper in my ear, 'It's time.' Either that, or just grab hold of me and drag me out of here … kicking and screaming."

No one ever did.

Once he established himself as a newspaper writer, Gene became a sought-after weapon in Denver's newspaper war. After he became Denver's premier local columnist, the *Post* tried to lure him away from the *News*. But he stayed put, and so did his fans.

A 1983 *News* feature that profiled some of Denver's most important institutions failed to mention Gene. Readers deluged the paper with complaints about the omission.

"I'm not sure I am an institution," he replied, "but I know some people who believe I belong in one."

He was regularly honored by Colorado community and humanitarian groups for his generosity and was beloved by his peers.

At a celebrity roast in 1983 before the National Conference of Christians and Jews, Dottie Lamm, a *Post* columnist and wife of then-Governor Dick Lamm, said of him:

"Gene really was a pioneer in radio. He was the first one to be turned off. Often, when I listen to him talk on the radio, I wonder how he can talk all morning without ever stopping to think.

"Gene really has a strange and wonderful program. The music's wonderful and he's strange."

Tom Gavin, a close friend and also a *Post* columnist, said Gene won the brotherhood award "not only for all the good things he's done professionally and for the community through a lot of years, but because as those who know him will attest, he is the real article, a genuinely fine person."

Journalism organizations honored Gene many times for his writing—a direct, no-frills brand that wasted no words.

Gene was hired at the *News* after Gavin jumped ship to the *Post.* Then-Editor Michael Balfe Howard said he was listening to KVOD while taking a bath at 2 a.m. when he had the "intuitive thought" that Gene would be exactly what the *News* needed.

"There was nothing tentative about Gene Amole," Howard said. "That's the foremost thing you could say about him. He wrote what he wanted to write and he wrote it well."

Gene wrote about his style in 1982: "Readers of this column know how devoted I am to linguistic simplicity. It is frequently alleged my copy reads more like a telegram than a newspaper column. I intend to keep it that way. There is a lot of competition for your attention in the morning."

He made it clear he didn't like long, run-on sentences, phrases crammed with adjectives and adverbs, or anything written by John Updike.

"He gives me more detail than I want or need," Gene wrote of the famous American novelist. "His sentences are of interminable length.

" … I tried again last week to read John Updike. My legs twitched. I wanted to run out in the street and scream. For me, reading John Updike is like passing a kidney stone."

In 1997, still championing simplicity, he wrote:

"The way some people write you know right away they are trying to impress you. They use big words and foreign terms in long sentences so you will think they are smart."

He quoted a newspaper editor whose name he couldn't remember: "Write to express not to impress."

"My father put it another way: 'Don't try to put the silk pants on anyone.' "

In addition to his terse lead paragraphs and spare prose, Gene regularly employed another literary device: the Idea Fairy. He introduced her to readers on Nov. 15, 1979, in a column that began with a warning from an editor never to write about column-writing—even when he had no idea what to write a column about.

"I have my very own Idea Fairy," he wrote. "She has been giving me material for years. That's why I have never stooped to writing a column about writing a column."

Every so often from then on, the Idea Fairy would appear in an Amole column, and together, the fairy and the writer would tango through a topic or situation.

An almost photographic memory for detail enriched Gene's columns with sights, sounds and smells—even 60 years later.

In 1990, reminiscing about Denver summers, he wrote:

"People from all over town took the No. 5 streetcar to Wash Park to swim in the lake. There were always a few kids on the bank of the lily pond, using bits of fresh beef liver to catch crawdaddies. Out on the neighborhood sidewalks little girls were skipping rope and chanting, 'Down by the ocean, down by the sea, Johnny broke a bottle and blamed it on me.'

"Old men stopped by the Broadway Creamery for all the buttermilk they could drink for a nickel. Old women picked choke cherries and wild plums along the banks of Cherry Creek and carried them home in brown paper grocery sacks."

Gene was forever proud of Denver, and he resisted the notion that the city had to import skyscrapers, traffic jams, a sprawling airport and thousands of new residents to better itself.

In 1996 he reminded readers why:

"The thing I like about the National Western (Stock Show) is that it's unique to Denver. It's not something we imitate from some other city. It takes us back to our roots. We really are an overgrown cow town."

Some people laughed at Gene, saying he was a myopic old-timer trying to turn the clock back to the 1950s.

Gene was largely a lone voice against the construction of Denver International Airport. He foretold the cost overruns, construction delays and real estate speculation that would dog DIA.

"In a way, he forced us to work harder, to rethink our ideas and strategies, to be sure we were absolutely convinced we were taking appropriate actions," said former Mayor Federico Peña, with whom Gene dueled over DIA. "Gene Amole had extraordinary insight. He cared deeply about the city and the people in this city. He had to be listened to."

His blunt opposition irritated airport supporters, among them Park Hill residents numbed by the noise of hundreds of jets taking off and landing daily at nearby Stapleton Airport.

Denver's political and business establishment, from Peña and Governor Roy Romer to the Greater Denver Chamber of Commerce, dismissed Gene's opposition as the views of a romantic blind to the city's emerging role in the global marketplace.

While Gene railed against DIA, the newspaper, on its editorial page, strongly supported building it. Gene treasured the freedom the *News* gave him to write what he wanted, ripping the corporate donations that fueled the airport push.

"Throughout all this," he recalled in 1995, "the Greater Denver Corp. brass was making regular calls on the *Rocky Mountain News* to shut me up. I met with platoons of angry lawyers, CEOs, bank presidents and other big enchiladas. They huffed, they puffed, but they didn't blow my house down.

" ... The purpose of this column is to give credit where credit is due. By golly, there would be no inflated air fares, no trouble-plagued baggage system, no $70 cab fares, no usurious bond interest payments, no jammed terminal trains, no leaky roof, no expansive soil, no cracked floors, no monster municipal bond debt, no DIA without the GDC."

Despite the bluntness he sometimes used as a bludgeon, Gene was a self-deprecating public figure.

A 1979 *Post* story on Gene called him "a gentlemanly, nonchalant, unpretentious sort who is the co-proprietor of KVOD-FM, a gentle, nonchalant, unpretentious radio station."

He was a blue-jeans-and-loafers businessman and craftsman.

During his 70s, infirmities rained in on Gene. He became blind in one eye, suffered a cataract in another and underwent numerous surgeries. For a time, he walked haltingly through the newsroom pulling his own oxygen tank.

He rarely wrote about his physical infirmities, except perhaps to chuckle at himself: "I can't see or hear very well anymore, but thank God I can still drive."

Toward the end, his frail body racked with pain, Gene still could not contain his excitement for work and life in the newsroom.

"It will be a while before I regain my health," he wrote on Father's Day 1997 in an extended column exploring love and pain.

"I have lost 40 pounds, but I am determined to get out and around again. I want to take Trish on a nice trip somewhere. I want to walk along Bear Creek with my little grandson, Jacob. I want to experience again my beloved, bright blue October. So many blessings, so much love in my life.

"Tomorrow?

"Tomorrow, I'm going back to work."

It's time to write the final chapter

CHILLED.

It's time to quit fooling around. No more "Gene Amole is taking a few days off," or "Gene Amole is on vacation. His column will resume when he returns," or "Gene Amole is off today. His column in Rocky Talk will resume Wednesday."

I suspect many of you have known all along my days here are numbered. Indeed they are. I am dying. I really don't know how much time I have left, but I didn't want to continue struggling in private and pretending that everything is OK.

I finally reached the point where I realized that there is no cure for the many ailments nibbling away at what is left of my life. The truth is I will die of multi-systems failure. Hey, I have fought my share of battles against the inevitable. I am 78, well past what many consider the optimum retirement age of 65.

Still, I am not retiring, just taking on a new assignment. I'm going to write a diary of my experience and share it with you. The idea came to me during one of my long hospital nights while I was cursing away at the pain.

How many other old folks were feeling what I felt, not knowing or understanding what the hell was happening to us? There are others as furious as I at insurance companies that hide behind unfeeling computerized telephone machines.

My diary is not going to be a maudlin self-serving bunch of glop. Some of it may even be amusing, like my discovery of the elevated toilet seat, for example. I wish it all could be funny, but it isn't. I'd have a best seller on my hands if I could write *The Joy of Dying*, but I can't.

I made the decision to quit fighting for my life every inch of the way after long talks with my family. When it comes to them, every other consideration comes in at a poor second place. My God, how I love them!

My wife, Trish, has been an angel through all this. My daughters, Tustin (aka Muffy) and Susan, have always been a great source of love and affection. My sons, Brett and Jon, are fine, strong men of whom any father could be proud, as is my son-in-law, Gary Waters.

And then, of course, there is my grandson, Jacob. There are no words to describe my love for him. My only regret is that I shall not live to see him flourish into manhood.

I'll say it again: My God, how I love them!

I am in a home-care hospice program, which means I won't take any medication to cure me, but only to make me more comfortable, to ease my pain. It would serve no purpose here to list all my ailments, but they are sufficient to justify my decision.

Suicide? Sure. I thought a lot about it but ruled it out. I didn't want to leave a mess for my family to clean up. I believe the old saying that suicide really is a permanent solution to what may be only a temporary problem. Something to think about for those who contemplate self-destruction as a solution to emotional or financial problems.

My diary won't just be about death and dying, but as soon as I get better control of my hands and quit shaking so much, I shall write about other stuff that interests me. Right now, though, it is about all I can do to punch out a complete sentence that is not garbled. There is medication that helps me with this. It is called Propranocol in 10-milligram tablets. I can pop up to four of these babies a day.

It might have been a violation of professional medical ethics when our family physician, Dr. Jeanne Day Seibert, gave Trish and me a nice little hug in her office after we made the decision to stop trying to cure my ills. I bubbled up a bit at that.

That's about it. Our editor, John Temple, has been darn nice about all this and he has my gratitude. I cherish our friendship and value his leadership at the dear old *Rocky* that means so much to me.

One other thing: I am going to tippy toe off the wagon next week for a single Tanqueray gin martini, extra-dry Martini & Rossi vermouth, two pimento-stuffed olives on a World's Fair round toothpick in a glacially-chilled stem glass.

Cheers!

October 31

More October gold for memory bank

COMFORT.

What can I do for an encore? Not easy, considering I announced in my last column Saturday I am dying. It's easier than you might think, though, because I woke up that morning to enjoy one of the brightest, most beautiful days of my life.

What a sparkling, October morning it was. This October is certainly no disappointment. As I have written before, it would be OK with me if we had 12 Octobers.

The view from our kitchen window is remarkable. It's all rolling green, dappled with gold trees all the way to the deep morning shadows of the foothills. And the air! Crisp. Clean and clear as Chablis.

Octobers are so special with the homey aroma of fresh-baked Jonathan apple pies with cinnamon bubbling up through the golden lattice crust. Is there anything better than that?

Anyhow, in case you missed that column, I wrote I was fed up with fighting a losing battle against all the ailments that have been nagging at me for years, and that I was ready to die.

After long talks with my family and my physician, I decided to become a patient of Hospice of Metro Denver. That means I will cease taking medication to try to cure my many ailments. Would you believe I was trying to gag down 15, sometimes more, pills every morning?

I became weary of dry-heaving. No more of that. Now, the only medication I take is for pain control. Hospice calls it "comfort care." It's working pretty well.

If I collapse, my family won't call 911. Just let me die with as much peace and comfort as possible. Several years ago I signed a document that states I don't want CPR or any mechanical method of resuscitation.

I already knew the drill because my wife Trish, who is a registered nurse, retired last year as Hospice Volunteer Coordinator for Exempla Health Care at Lutheran Medical Center. She has been wonderfully supportive through all of this. Making this decision relieved me of a monstrous burden I had been bearing for years.

What a nice bunch of family and friends I have! Showing up on my doorstep Saturday morning was *Rocky* editor John Temple with a gift from my pals in the newsroom: two classic martini glasses.

Dusty Saunders' interview on Channel 4 was warm and wonderful. And did you see Chuck Green's Sunday column in *The Denver Post?* What a nice thing for him to do. For years, readers have been trying to cast us as mortal enemies simply because we work for different newspapers. It was never true.

I don't know how much longer I will live. I am hoping for another October, but if doesn't work out that way, that's OK. I have so many beautiful ones in my memory bank. I want to write some more about the changing seasons in the next couple of my columns. There are many other thoughts about dying I want to share with you if you care to read them.

Of course it is way too early to think about casseroles and covered dishes. It was nice, though, of neighbors Doris and Harry Schack to drop off a banana-nut bread. Doris makes the best banana-nut bread on the planet. And it was dear of my old friend Kathy Recor Habas to bring a little companion for the Idea Fairy. We have yet to hear from her.

On Friday, I want to write about funerals.

November 2

Savoring the dear and the familiar

Just because I love October so much doesn't mean I think less of dear old November, at least the first part of it.

How pleasant it was Sunday to watch little Jacob running through the thicket of elms, maples and cottonwoods along Bear Creek with his Uncle Jon, my No. 2 son.

It was at about that same spot all those years ago I took Susan, Jacob's mom, to play when she was also just 5. Every evening I took her and as many neighborhood kids as we could find to play on the swing set, the merry-go-round and the slides.

Then we'd go to Baskin-Robbins for ice cream to smear all over the back of the old family station wagon. Years later, I'd take our dog, Oreo, to frisk through the fallen leaves so she could jump into frigid Bear Creek to break the ice and chase ducks.

This November has its charms, too. Mr. King Le transplanted some tiny shrubs in our back yard that have turned a brilliant crimson, the reddest red I have ever seen. Don't know what they are.

Speaking of color, did you see that movie, *Meet Joe Black?* The critics didn't think much of it, but I liked it every much. It was a remake of that old black-and-white movie in the 1930s called *Death Takes A Holiday.*

Frederick March played the role of death to find out what it was like to be alive. In the new version, death is named Joe Black and is played by Brad Pitt. He is sent to tell a financier, played by Anthony Hopkins, that he is going to die.

Of course there is a subplot of death falling in love with the financier's daughter, but the real thrust of the story is how the old man deals with the knowledge of his impending death.

So you can understand why I was attracted to the story. If Joe Black were to come to my house this morning, Trish would have to tell him: "I'm sorry, Mr. Black, you'll have to come back. My husband is just too busy to die today."

And indeed I am. Busy isn't the word for it, maybe "overwhelmed" better describes my situation. Hospice of Metro Denver nurses, the social worker and chaplain have all made contact with Trish and me.

Old friends from all over are calling, including Max DiJulio, who crooned to me over the phone, "I'll be seeing you again in all those old familiar places, my heart embraces ..." All of that in his cracked Italian dialect only a few can understand.

John Temple suggested I explain how my feelings about death have evolved over the years. As a teen-age soldier in World War II, I wasn't afraid to die, I just didn't want it to hurt. Now I am an old man ready to die because it hurts too much to live. Does that make any sense?

Even with the pain, I am savoring all the days left to me. They are such wonderful days. I see family and friends in a dimension I had not perceived before. Maybe that's what makes them so precious. I am finding treasure where I thought none existed.

My philosophy has always been living one day at a time. That really hasn't changed. Now, though, I am relishing each one, not just living them.

Oh yes, I don't want a funeral. I'll explain why another day.

November 5

Still so much to do and see, if only I had the energy

DARTASS.

How did we used to say it? I remember: Too pooped to pop. Am I ever. That little outing last week at the park with Trish, Susan, Gary and

5

Jacob just about washed me out. All I did was sit down and watch Jacob play for about 45 minutes. There is no question about it, I'm getting weaker all the time.

So much so, that I am afraid I won't be able to see as many old friends as I would like. Even my own family. Muffy and Susan wanted to plan a little outing this week at White Fence Farm. You know the place. It's out on West Jewell Avenue, across from Green Gables.

We love the fried chicken there, big platters of it, served family style, but I was too weak to make it. Then they thought about carrying it out, but I think that large a family event would be too much, too. I'll pull myself together, though, for Thanksgiving, which Susan will do this year. I hope I'll make it to Christmas for our annual Christmas brunch.

What a blast that is! We have Hickory Baked Ham, scrambled eggs, sausage, bagels and lox, corned beef hash, pastries you wouldn't believe, fresh fruit plate, cheap champagne and a lot of other stuff.

I raise the issue about my fatigue because so many old friends want to come "see" me, and frankly, these visits just tire me too much. I hope they understand. Frankly, I'm not much to look at now, anyhow.

My weight has dropped to 135 pounds, down somewhat from my regular 170. I weigh now what I weighed when I was drafted in the Army. You know how soldiers are about giving guys nicknames based on their appearance. Right off the bat I became known as "Dartass Amole."

So I hope old friends understand that I love them and am eager to talk to some on the phone when I am not sacking out, or read their cards and letters. Trying to see all of them is just too difficult for the time being. Maybe I'll get some strength back. I hope so.

The phone has presented a problem, though. My arm is so weak I can only hold it up to my ear for a short time. My son Brett has rigged up a headset hooked to a wireless phone that works pretty well.

I am genuinely sorry my flippant remark about writing a book called *The Joy of Dying* has upset one of my readers. I suspect as time passes others will be angry, too, at some of my feelings about death and dying.

I have never believed there is a hell and a heaven in the hereafter. I have had my share of heaven and hell in my life and don't expect any more. So far as I know, I get to die only once, and I'll just have to do it my own way.

I could be wrong, as readers have noted I have been in the past. I once shared my beliefs about the afterlife with a dear friend, Sister Mary

Louise "Lamb Chop" Beutner, a Roman Catholic nun and world-famous Shakespeare scholar.

When I told her I didn't believe in heaven, she said, "Boy, do you ever have a nice surprise waiting for you!"

If she's right, I hope she'll be there to greet me at the pearly gates.

November 7

Big wheels keep on rollin'

REFLECTIONS.

"It's gone, now." It was my son Jon's voice on the telephone. He called to say he had sold my 1965 Ford pickup truck. I hated to see it go, but where I am going, I won't have any use for an old pickup truck.

I bought it in 1970-something from Dick Bott, a friend of Beth Koepke, daughter of my business partner, Ed Koepke. Dick Stevens had told me every man in his lifetime ought to have at least one pickup truck. He was right about that.

No telling what the mileage is on that old baby, but it must be pushing 300,000. I loved that truck. It served my family and friends very well over the years. Jon drove it the most. Muffy drove it back and forth from Aspen when she lived there. Brett hauled stuff around in it. Trish even drove it every now and then.

The gang at the radio station used it to move to different apartments and to haul washing machines and refrigerators and stuff for our old DSO Marathon fund-raiser. Our fashion department at the *Rocky* even used it to illustrate a fashion shoot it was doing for a Sunday spread.

Jon and I had just restored it for the third time. It originally was a sort of turquoise color, like an Easter egg. Since I bought it, I have had it painted red three times. You should have seen it. New chrome wheels. New rubber. New glass. Gorgeous. He said the guy who bought it seemed like he'll take care of it.

"It sounded so good when he drove it away," Jon said, and then he was quiet for a few seconds, and then he said, "It was something we did together."

Enough, already, with the weepy stuff. I was overwhelmed by the torrent of e-mail good wishes flooding into the *Rocky*. I don't deserve even one-thousandth of the nice things readers have been sending, but I am going to read all of them anyhow, every one.

There have been hundreds and hundreds, so many I haven't been able to count. Most have been very supportive, but not all. For example, Dimitri writes, "This seems like more of your schmaltzy grandstanding. Why not keep something like this private?"

Names of some wonderful old friends are popping up, like Jocko Samson, brother of Charley. We all worked at the old KVOD. He remembers the Christmas Blizzard of '82 during which he and I were snowbound in the KVOD studios. "For 18 straight hours, Geno 'n Jocko made sure listeners heard every conceivable version of 'Joy to the World,'" he writes. "Including the Boston Pops Live with Bert Parks. I have great memories, but that one has scarred me for life. I still can't listen to Christmas music in any form."

How nice it was to hear from Gabby Stern. She and I sat at the same pod in the old *Rocky*. What a great journalist she has become. I still can't believe a boob of an assistant city editor we had at the time couldn't see that and let Gabby slip through our fingers. She is currently a London-based correspondent for *The Wall Street Journal*.

I was flattered Don Kinney devoted so much of his Channel 6 program Friday to my work over the years. Don stands alone in the video documentary world. He has no equal. I have been privileged to work with him on many of his "Rocky Mountain Reflections" projects.

And I want to thank you all so much for your kind thoughts. Your support means a great deal to me and our family. It is a debt we never can repay.

November 9

Of staying busy and writing obits

CRAZY.

The trick is to stay busy. Just sitting around and waiting to die is for the birds. If I had my 'druthers, I'd 'druther I'd had a nice painless terminal stroke while I was asleep at night. It hasn't turned out that way, though.

That's OK. I'm doing all right. But again, the trick is to stay busy. Thank God, I still have my job. I am told it is something of a rarity for someone in hospice care to still be working. In addition to my columns, other stuff is keeping me busy.

For example, the very Saturday morning when my story about dying was in the *Rocky*, I had a phone call from my old friend, David Yeakley. "Gene," he said, "before you check out, I want you to write my obituary."

He went on to explain that he had never married, had no children or other family, no one to tidy up after he dies. Of course I knew all of this. We have been friends for maybe 40 years. I guess I never thought much about who would take care of Dave's affairs after he "checks out."

This does not appear to be an imminent probability. He is 11 years younger than I and appears to be in excellent health. Dave is a retired interior designer, and a fine one at that. Among other things, he headed the Interior Design Department at the University of Denver.

He stopped by the house the next day with information he wanted in his obituary. It was pretty spare stuff. There was nothing about the many awards and honors he has received. It was just sort of "Dave-was-here-and-now-he-is-gone" kind of thing.

So, I wrote it just as he wanted it, even though I thought it deserved what we call "feature obit" treatment. I was happy to do it for him. He helped make our home look very special with his design skills.

He's been such a good friend, too. Some years back when I was going through the tortures of the damned with neck reconstruction surgery, Dave scouted around and found me a bed I could sleep on with some degree of comfort.

How did I meet Dave? Probably through Betty Ambler or Carla Frank, two other dear friends of mine. Seems like Dave, Betty and I did the martini thing at the old BI tavern on Colorado Boulevard.

Yes, I finally had my martini, at least half of one. Wow! You never forget something like that. My mention of it in the column prompted a letter from Del Plested, my friend for more than 50 years. "At 93, Geno, your 78 years seem so young to even think of checking out," she writes. "But I'll be thinking of you every night when I lift my single glass of bourbon and water."

We shared what she called "some of the incredible, crazy, wonderful times our KMYR gang had together." That was the little 250-watt radio station where many of our careers began. Del was a copy writer and later program director after Pat Kidder left.

Del went on to bigger and better things in life and became a correspondent for the prestigious *Women's Wear Daily*. She and her sister, Alice, were born in Trinidad, that wonderful Colorado town that was so rich in Spanish-American heritage.

I tend to wander some in these columns. I guess I'll write again in this diary about how I am keeping busy because I have run out of space this time. In the meantime, though, I want it understood that I am not going back into the obituary-writing business. Just Dave's, that's all.

November 12

Family, fans make me 'luckiest dying man alive'

ALONE.

Folks are curious but don't want to appear tactless. They just don't know how to ask me how much longer I will live. The truth is I just don't know. There is a sort of hospice rule of thumb, though. Patients usually live for about six months after they enter the program.

When I look in the mirror each morning, it seems to me my death may come sooner than that. I have lost so much weight due to my inability to eat because my throat is constricted. Drinking water is even difficult.

There is a procedure to open my throat some. It's called esophageal dilatation. It's a sort of roto-rooter process that reams out my gullet. That will certainly help. I have promised John Temple that he and I will split a hot pastrami sandwich on pumpernickel before I die.

In the meantime, I am trying to tidy up my affairs a little each day. I am sorry I'll never see the newsroom again. I have always said that everyone has to be somewhere, and my somewhere is the newsroom. In these last years it has been my life away from home.

I keep telling young reporters that these are the good old days, but they don't believe me. Someday they may understand. What a great adventure my life has been at the *Rocky!*

I dreaded cleaning out my desk. Imagine, 24 years of crud. As luck would have it, I never had to clean it out, but my daughter, Tustin, did volunteer to do the dirty work. She knew where to start because she was a reporter for the *Rocky* for nine years.

What a joy it was for me to be able to work in the same newsroom with her. Now, she is public information officer for the Cherry Creek School District, a job she really loves. Anyhow, she and Lynn Bartels boxed up everything last Saturday and left it on my front porch.

My son-in-law, Gary Waters, then toted the boxes down to the basement and put them in the corner with other boxes we never opened when we moved into this house seven years ago.

I have started cleaning out my closet. Don't have much use for clothing anymore. Mostly, I wear Nike sweats that Trish buys for me. They are so much more comfortable than even jeans. Imagine me, dressed like a jock.

I am convinced I am the luckiest dying man still alive. I have had such wonderful support from Trish, my sons and daughters, old friends, readers of my columns and my many friends at the *Rocky Mountain News.*

I can't imagine what it must be like for old folks dying alone with no one to help them. This reminds me of something Fred Hobbs told me when we worked together at the old KDEN many years ago. He was doing a radio documentary on the problems elderly people face each day.

Fred said he noticed many seniors living alone would cover their telephones with something so they would be out of sight. They didn't want to be reminded that the telephone would never ring and no one would ever call to ask how they were getting along. No one would ever say on the telephone, "I love you."

November 14

Pain, pain, go away: hospice is a blessing

PAIN.

Somewhere along the line I wrote that I didn't want it to hurt when I die. Pain is a big issue with me, as I know it must be for others. That doesn't mean, however, I am in constant agony.

Pain is not new to me. I have been struggling with arthritis for many years. I have also had back and neck surgery that has left me with pain. Since the end of World War II, I have been treated for peripheral neuropathy that affects my hands and feet.

It probably was a result of my service in the Battle of the Bulge in World War II where so many of us were afflicted with frostbite. Peripheral neuropathy is also prevalent among diabetics and people who are suffering from AIDS.

These aches and pains have come home to roost here at the end of my life. I have never been able to use aspirin or any medication containing aspirin, as well as most oral steroids, because they cause my stomach to bleed.

It is fortunate for me that hospice care is dedicated to pain management. I don't know how I would get along without it. Chronic-pain sufferers know how elusive pain can be. One day it can be unbearable, and the next it almost disappears.

There is a wide array of medications to deal with pain. Not all are appropriate for everyone. In my case, I get the best relief from Roxanol-T. It's an oral morphine sulfate solution from concentrate.

I also use Roxicet, which is a liquid form of Percocet. I used Percocet in tablet form in the past, but now it is too difficult to swallow because of my constricted throat. Another weapon in my arsenal against pain is the Duragesic patch, or Fentanyl Transdermal System.

It is a patch that adheres to the skin as do patches to stop smoking and to cure other ailments. They come in different strengths and are generally changed every 72 hours. They have worked very well for me, but I understand their use is limited because, as death nears, patients tend to lose weight and have less tissue available to absorb the medication.

These are the prescribed medications I am currently using, and they are serving me well. However, there are other strategies that work for me, too.

Massage therapy tops the list. I am a firm believer in professionally administered massage.

My certified therapist is Angie Aufdemberge. I swear there is magic in her fingers as she makes the pain all but disappear for a time from my feet, hips, calves, shoulders and neck. She also has a bachelor's degree in biology. Before I became terminally ill, Angie was my personal trainer, a skill in which she is also certified.

I also have two pieces of Homedco equipment that have served me well. One is a lounge chair I bought at Costco. It was actually dirt cheap. My son, Jon, put it together. It vibrates in alternate pulses from my ankles all the way up to my neck.

The other is a reflexology gizmo Muffy gave me. Like the chair, it pulses with varied intensities through my feet into my legs as I sit down. It's great when I wake up in the middle of the night in stabbing foot pain. I can spend a few minutes on the gizmo, and I can get back to sleep.

I know this doesn't mean much to most readers, but I hope this information may help others who are suffering as I am.

November 16

Folks struggle to find the right thing to say

BRIGHT LIGHT.

The phone rang just as Trish and I were sitting down for a bowl of soup. It was a guy from the Communications Workers of America, the union with which the Denver Newspaper Guild has an affiliation.

"Mr. Am-hole," he said, "I would like to make an appointment with you to visit your family and explain an opportunity available to you as a member of the Denver Newspaper Guild to save you money on life insurance."

Well, I almost busted out laughing at the idea of a company that would be willing to sell life insurance to a dying man. I didn't let him make his pitch any longer and just flat out told him I was dying.

I probably was too blunt in describing my situation. He obviously had no idea who I am or that I was keeping a diary about getting ready to die. After I blurted it out, I was sorry right away I had been so insensitive to his feelings.

The poor guy struggled with what to say. He mumbled something about how he hoped I would find eternal peace in heaven, or something like that. Then we hung up. It was another instance of how folks struggle to find the right thing to say.

It's not easy for me, either. Some are kind enough to say they will miss me. My automatic response would be to say, "I'll miss you, too," but that seems inappropriate. It's an open question of whether I'll be in a position to miss anyone or anything.

I suppose that's one of the things about dying that makes it such a unique adventure. Sure, I'm curious. Aren't we all? What about all those near-death experiences folks have reported about the bright light at the end of the tunnel?

Some people who are dying don't want to be left alone. I remember it was that way when my friend Starr Yelland died. I'd visit him as often as I could at the Hospice of Metro Denver residence where he spent his final days.

I would try to spend some time with him so his wife could get away for an hour or so. He seemed to need her all the time. He was quite confused toward the end. He'd say to me, "Geno, I don't know what I am doing here."

I don't mind being alone. I need to be alone for a little quiet reflection. It is also important for me that Trish have an opportunity to get away from the house for her fitness training, to get her hair trimmed, or to do some shopping or have lunch with old friends.

Sure, I wish I had more time to see my old pals, but I don't. Visitors take so much out of me, and I want to spend as much time as I can with my family. I haven't even seen any of my old buddies at KVOD, my home away from home for all those years on Ruby Hill.

That's OK. They have moved on to more fulfilling lives and they know I wish them well. I talk on the phone every week or so to Ed Koepke, my business partner for more than four decades. I don't expect him to come to see me. He's 82 now, and it's stressful to drive all the way across town. He knows I understand this.

I did have a pleasant telephone chat the other day with *Rocky* film critic Robert Denerstein. He was news editor when I came to work here in 1977. There is no more talented a writer at our newspaper. Bob can literally do anything in our newsroom, anything. I always thought he should be a columnist and probably a better one than I have been, but then that wouldn't be too tough.

I have always said anyone can do what I do.

November 19

As the indignities come to visit, one must laugh

TRICKY.

Comfort is the name of the game. My Hospice of Metro Denver advisers are devoted to keeping me comfortable. There's more to it than that. They want me to be careful. It is an absolute must. When I am walking, I have to concentrate on every step. At this point, walking is risky business.

My greatest fear is that I will fall and break my hip and have to return to the hospital where it is doubtful I would ever recover. So what? So I am going to die anyhow. Well, the "so what" is that I want to be comfortable as long as I can, and wasting away in a hospital is no way to be comfortable.

Our house is a lovely older home, but it is fraught with danger if I'm not careful. It's a two-story house with a basement. There are 28 stair steps from top to bottom. It is tricky negotiating them with a cane and 50 feet of oxygen hose hanging from my snoot.

So you can see why concentration is so important. I can't let my mind wander even while making my way to the john. And speaking of that, I had no idea there was such a thing as an elevated toilet seat until my body started wasting away.

It was during my last hospital stay that I began to notice the regular toilet seat was too large for my skinny, old keester. Get the picture? (If this is a little more than you want to know, feel free to bug out now and look at the brassiere ads.)

Anyhow, I took my problem to my resourceful son, Brett, and with Trish's guidance, he went shopping and came home with an elevated toilet seat. Voila! Keester comfort! He also bought a bedside commode I hope I shall never have to use.

I hope you can see the humor in these indignities. I have to be able to laugh at myself. I want to emulate my old friend Pat Haggerty who died of prostate cancer. His twin sister, Patricia, a Roman Catholic nun, was with him when he died. She said, "Pat, the priest is here to give you your last rites."

He was barely able to open his eyes but whispered, "Do I have to tip this guy?" What a nifty way to go.

On an earlier chapter in this diary, I wrote about the drugs to lessen my pain. There are consequences, or side effects, of those—one being constipation, the other, dry skin.

Hospice recommended Neosporyn for dry skin in sensitive areas. For me, though, I found Albertson's Skin Therapy a better idea. The emulsion is thinner and it absorbs more quickly.

I am writing these columns more frequently than they are appearing in the *Rocky*. Jim Trotter, our assistant managing editor, is keeping track of them.

Of late, though, I have been asking myself, "Why am I keeping this diary?"

I had hoped it might help others, but now I'm not so sure. Dying is very personal and each of us must find his or her own way. Are folks still reading them, or are they getting fed up and want me to shut up?

Are they entertaining as well as informational? I have always believed personal commentary ought to have some kind of entertainment quality to it.

I don't know. I'll just keep on cranking them out as long as I can. That's the thing I do, and I'll just keep on doing it. OK?

November 20

Continuing to work an easy decision

BLISS.

My friend and *Rocky* Editor John Temple wanted to know how I came to my decision to go public with entering hospice. It probably has more to do with my work than anything else.

The made-up word of workaholic comes to mind. I have been working since age 14. It's not just because of necessity. I like to work. After caring for my family, work has been the meaning of my life.

It was that way when I started as a kid janitor, then an elevator operator, a hotel lobby porter and bellboy, a disc jockey, a soldier, a radio and TV newsman, a filmmaker, public relations flack, advertising copywriter, a small magazine publisher and, in recent years, a columnist. I liked it all.

It wasn't the recognition or the money I loved. It was the work itself. When it became apparent I was going to die in the not-too-distant future, I wanted to keep doing the thing I love as long as I could.

I know that doesn't make sense to a lot of people who look upon what we do as drudgery, but that's the way I feel about it. In looking back on it all, I am so grateful I have been able to pursue my "bliss," as Joseph Campbell wrote.

So, if I am going to continue to work until the last breath, I might as well write about something close to me. After all, column-writing is personal commentary.

It sure beats sitting here and writing thumb-suckers about terrorism, T-Rex, anthrax and other subjects about which I know next to nothing. I am learning how to die, however, and that's why I decided to go public with what is happening to me.

John was also curious about other people's feelings about what is left of my life. There are no words to describe how humbled I am from the outpouring of love and support from folks I don't even know and also from my old friends and pals here at the *Rocky*. I sit here and read the messages, look at the videotapes and bawl like a baby. I know it may seem sissy to react that way, but that's the way I feel.

He also wondered if I have any advice for people who want to talk to others in my situation. Just be yourself. Brett took me over to Tom and Jake's for a haircut last week. One of the barbers is an old-car nut as I am, and he wanted to know how I felt about selling my 1965 Ford pickup.

He had read about it in my column. I was glad he asked me. It was something we had in common. There was no reason to get weepy about it. It was just a couple of old guys talking about something both cared about.

John wondered how active is my life of the mind. I'm not sure I understand the question. I do think about many things other than dying, though. For example, my 5-year-old grandson, Jacob, occupies much of my thought.

What better way to end my life than by thinking about the promise in store for him in his life. My friend, Tom Gavin, put it well when he said, "Jacob is your pathway to the future." Old Tom sure has a way with words, doesn't he?

In my mind's eye, I can see him pitching left-handed in a baseball game, playing the violin in front of a great symphony orchestra, visiting Trish after I am gone, having adventures all over the world and living his life to its full measure.

Sure, there are times when I am confused, forgetful and sad, but I'm not angry about dying. My mind is still clicking along on most of its cylinders. I hope so.

November 21

Making the best of 'precious few'

SQUEAKY.

It seems like an oxymoron to stay healthy when you know you are going to die. What's the use? Why not say to hell with it and just go ahead and die? I never felt that way, even for an instant.

Kurt Weill's "September Song" comes to mind and the part of the lyric that speaks of how the "days narrow down to a precious few." My God, I wish I had written that. Anyhow, now that my days are narrowing down to a precious few, I want to make the best of them.

I have found a special happiness I had not experienced before. They are filled with love from my family, friends and those special folks with whom I have worked at Mother *Rocky*.

Mother *Rocky*? Yes, that was the name Bob Stapp used when he, Jack Frank and I exchanged chuckles over the Denver Press Club's noontime bill of fare.

Old Stapper and Jack were two of the best funny writers ever to work in this town.

When Jack was dying down in Florida, I wrote his obituary before the fact so he could enjoy it before he went to the Great Newsroom in the Sky. Come to think of it, that's what a lot of pals have been doing for me.

Wow, did I ever get off the track or what? I started out by making the best of what time I have left. I do tend to ramble, don't I? Reminds me of that old New Orleans funeral march, "Oh, Didn't He Ramble?"

Getting back to square one, I am trying my best to stay as healthy as I can. It's not easy. I have lost so much weight. I am down to 130 now, some 40 pounds less than I weighed just a few months ago.

When we bought this house seven or eight years ago, I noticed my bathroom had full-length mirrors. I hate them. There is no way I can avoid seeing myself buck-naked as I get out of the shower. What a terrible shock that is.

I am so gaunt I remind myself of those poor Holocaust victims those of us in my old 6th Armored Division liberated from Buchenwald toward the end of World War II.

Now that I am getting my esophagus reamed out, I am going to try to eat more foods to restore some strength. I want to get back to meat and potatoes and what my dad called "barrel gravy."

Personal neatness has always been important to me. The first thing I do in the morning is make my own bed. Maybe it's a hangover from my soldiering days. Trish would be more than happy to do it for me, but I think it is important for me to do this and other personal needs myself.

It helps restore my sense of order, like paying my bills as soon as I receive them. I don't like to put off little chores. Maybe it's just foolish thinking, but I believe keeping up to speed on these things helps me maintain peace of mind.

Did someone say, "Cleanliness is next to Godliness?" I believe it. I want to be squeaky clean. When I had rehabilitation after my stroke several years ago, I had grab bars installed in my shower. I think everyone should have them in all showers. They are a great help to avoid accidental slipping.

I never skip a shower. I shave every day and will continue to do so until the end. These are just some of the things that help me make the best of my "precious few."

November 22

Funerals aren't my thing, really

IRREVERENT.

I don't like funerals and don't want one after I die. Of course I won't have anything to say about it. There is some difference of opinion in our family on this sensitive issue. They all know how I feel about this.

Muffy put it rather well when she said that funerals are not for the dead but for the living. I suspect my family will get together in our home for a private little memorial service of their own. That's OK by me, I just don't want a big carnival or circus.

Funerals have always been painful experiences for me, especially when I have been called upon to deliver the eulogy. I must be the all-time champion eulogy giver. A couple of years ago, I did a back-to-back—one for Sam Lusky and the other for Harry Farrar, both old friends.

Sam must have known how I felt about funerals because shortly before he died, he extracted a promise from his son, Mark, that I deliver the eulogy. How can you say no to a thing like that?

Funerals for old reporters used to be fun. They were irreverent, a shade cynical and rarely spiritual. Not anymore, though. Journalism has become serious business by serious young men and women who generally move on to more profitable pursuits when opportunity rears its lovely head.

My favorite eulogist was Jungle Jim Kelly. His were masterpieces that always left the congregation, regardless of denomination, roaring with laughter. Jungle Jim has himself gone to the Great Newsroom in the Sky, and no one has risen to succeed him.

Pocky Marranzino wrote great obituaries. Our own Frances Melrose once confided in me that when she dies, she wanted Pocky to write her obituary, but Pocky is up there with Jungle Jim, and Frances is outliving us all, bless her soul.

Several years go, Horan & McConaty opened a funeral service and cremation facility on South Wadsworth, not far from our home. Driving past it every day on my way to work and back home again, I decided to make arrangements for my cremation in advance to spare Trish that responsibility when I die.

I was comfortable with Horan & McConaty because Valerie Horan is an old friend and someone for whom I have great respect. Also, when Trish was doing hospice work for Lutheran Medical Center, she became acquainted with John Horan, who was very considerate and helpful to her in her work training volunteers.

Valerie is the daughter of Francis and Boots Vanderbur and the granddaughter of George W. Olinger, who founded Olinger mortuaries and was a member of the Highlander Boys, an organization that had a profound effect upon my life.

Until he died, I received a letter from Mr. Olinger on my birthday wherever in the world I happened to be. The family asked me to deliver the eulogy at his funeral and I was honored to do so.

Again, after all the wonderful and often undeserved things that have been said and written about me, I have no need of a funeral. I gave copies of my military records to Horan & McConaty, and they will arrange for my ashes to be interred at Fort Logan, where I became a soldier all those years ago. They will present Trish with a correctly folded Old Glory.

Everything that goes around, comes around.

November 23

Important to show love, support for the caregiver

THANKLESS.

When did all this business of victimization start? Was it back during the Vietnam War when folks started blaming everyone else for their problems? I didn't like it then and don't like it now.

In looking back on my life, I have generally deserved the bumps and bruises I have had along the way. On the other side of that coin, I haven't always deserved the good fortune I have had. As John Kennedy observed, "Life is unfair."

I have been thinking a lot about this lately as my time is winding down. What possible thing did Trish, my wife, ever do to deserve being my "caregiver"? That's the word hospice uses to identify the person in the home primarily responsible for the patient's 24-hour care.

The caregiver is part of the hospice team that includes the hospice medical director, a primary care nurse, a social worker, a certified nurse aide, the chaplain, a volunteer and a grief counselor.

Of course, not all these professionals are with the patient all the time, but the caregiver is. Getting back to the good fortune I have, and maybe don't deserve, Trish is a registered nurse, as I have written before. Until last year, she was volunteer coordinator for Exempla Hospice at Lutheran Medical Center.

Still, with all that going for her, taking care of me is no walk in the park. The longer I live, the more demanding her work will become. I am mostly able to care for myself when it comes to cleanliness. Not so, down the road. I will need her for more personal needs. This will be difficult for both of us.

Much of this goes unnoticed outside the family. We were pleased, though, when an old Bear Valley neighborhood friend did take notice of what Trish is doing for me. Doug Miller and his wife, Michelle, sent her a self-care basket filled with little reminders of the affection they hold for her. There were books, a little note pad, a CD of music she enjoyed all those years ago when the Millers lived just two doors away.

We were close to the Miller family. Doug and my son, Brett, are the same age and attended school together. They were involved in a perpetual whiffle-ball game in our backyard, a game of horse in the hoop over our garage door and a game of four-square on our driveway. The door was always open to Doug and always will be. I have often told him he is like a third son to me.

Caregiving can be a pretty thankless job. It isn't just the work alone. The aftermath must be difficult for the caregiver. When the patient dies, who will be there to fill the emptiness?

Sure, all the caregiving work will end. There will be some relief from that. Giving brings satisfaction, too, and that will be gone. How will the caregiver cope with loneliness? Will friends understand this, and will they exercise care in trying to alleviate the pain of loss? Will they do too much, be pushy and invade her need for privacy? Will they be sensitive enough to seek a balance between too little and too much?

What did I fail to do to prepare her for life after my death? How can I return even a little of the love she has given me all these many years when I have so little time left?

These questions haunt me and probably will until I finally die.

November 24

Thanksgiving trimmed with love

HIGHLIGHT.

If any of our family was thinking that this would be my last Thanksgiving, they didn't say so. It was on my mind, though, as Trish drove us up to Susan and Gary's house Thursday.

Thanksgiving has always been my favorite holiday. It makes no demands on us. We aren't required to purchase the affection of others with gifts. It is a day for families to come together, to share a meal, to laugh, to watch football, to go to sleep on the couch.

Susan was a little apprehensive about the dinner because she had soaked the turkey in brine before roasting it. It was something she had seen on TV, but she needn't have worried. The dinner was perfect.

Muffy's turkey stuffing was superb. She had taken my celebrated stuffing recipe and added some innovations of her own, like portobello mushrooms. I have always said you can't screw up turkey stuffing so long as you remember onions, celery and butter, or chicken stock.

It is interesting that so many readers who e-mailed me about my decision not to needlessly prolong my life, mentioned my turkey stuffing recipe. Imagine that. Immortality through turkey stuffing!

All other things considered, I loved the dinner for another reason: I didn't have to carve the bird. I have never been able to slice it artistically as represented in all those Norman Rockwell paintings we used to see on the cover of *The Saturday Evening Post*.

When I carved the turkey, it was sort of like wrestling two out of three falls with Stone Cold Steve Austin. But now that this apparently is my last Thanksgiving, the torch has been passed to Gary, my son-in-law.

Susan had a little ceremony before we ate. She had arranged eight small candles in a circle on a dinner plate, seven around the edge and one in the center, a candle representing each of us.

She asked us to each light our candle and say what we were thankful for.

After all the candles were lit, the plate was placed before our family picture on the buffet. When it was Jacob's turn, he said, "I am thankful for my parents and my pets." He thought a minute and then added, "I am thankful for God, too."

The highlight of the day was when Trish give Jacob the violin she had played when she was young. His kindergarten class had attended a Colorado Symphony Orchestra children's concert.

He came away from the concert fascinated with the violin. You should have seen his eyes and his smile when Trish handed him the violin. For the rest of the day, he didn't let it out of his sight. I asked him where he would keep it, and he took me into his room and placed the violin on his bed.

You should have seen him, walking from room to room, pulling the bow across the strings, trying to make music. It was pure joy.

I have to say, my grandson has made these last years of my life special. He is such a wise little boy. He is interested in everything. Will he be a left-handed relief pitcher, a golfer and a soccer player and a concert violinist all at the same time?

Is this just silly talk from an addled old grandfather? Hey, I get to do that. All old grandparents get to do that, don't they?

Thursday was certainly my last Thanksgiving Day. I couldn't have asked for a more loving one.

November 26

Strange 'presences,' dreams of Pop bring comfort

Respect.

You may be asking yourself if old Geno has gone loopy, or what? I raise the issue because I have been experiencing some presences. This means I sometimes perceive images that are not physically present.

They don't linger very long. They seem to flash on only for an instant. The strange thing about them is that they appear mostly in my right eye that has been totally blind for years.

They are indistinct, but generally have a human shape, mostly standing. They can be either male or female. They don't speak and make no sound at all. I am reporting this for whatever it may be worth. Consider it a part of my diary of dying.

This is not the first time I have had similar visions, if that is what they are. Years ago following my lung surgery, I "saw" human figures at my bedside in Porter Hospital.

They were much more clearly defined than those I have been having recently. They seemed ready to speak to me but disappeared before they could.

I asked my surgeon about them, and he said they were not uncommon among patients who have been anesthetized.

Did I write a column about them? I can't remember. There is so much stuff I can't remember anymore. I do remember what Hellie

Ferill said about memory loss, though: "The older I get, the better my forgetter gets."

My hospice nurse said these presences often occur to people who are dying. The closer the patient gets to death, the clearer these images often become. They are never frightening but usually have a calming effect. She also said most hospice patients experience what she described as "peace" before death.

I find I have been dreaming more, or at least I am remembering my dreams more than I had been. Many have been about my father. I can't recall ever dreaming about him before. I loved my father and he loved me.

However, he really didn't know how to be a father very well because his father didn't either. Without making this too complicated, my grandfather was a tough old guy, and my father was afraid of him. Not so with me, though. I think Grandpa must have realized what he missed with his son and showered his affection on me.

Anyhow, I welcome the dreams about Pop, as I called him. They seem to bring him closer to me now that I am dying than he ever was while both of us were still alive. Does this make any sense?

Trish has arranged photographs in our family room of me as a boy with both Grandpa and Pop. When I look at them, I seem to see more in them than I had ever seen before. They bring back a sense of warmth that make these last days of mine so rewarding.

Lately, folks have been sending me a lot of literature about dying. I appreciate the attention, but I prefer just going it alone with the emotional support I am getting from my family and friends. You can't know how important that has become to me.

Here I am writing about dying as so many others have done before me. The truth of it is that none of us really knows what it is like to die. I have no idea whether what I am writing will be of any help to others. I can only hope that it will. My intentions are good. I'm not trying to convert anyone to any belief. It is your right to privacy I totally respect.

Tearful goodbye succeeds in melting years away

TEARFUL.

I knew it wouldn't be easy to tell Dorothy I am dying. There was no other choice. I didn't want her to call here after I am dead, and Trish would have to tell her.

Do you remember Dorothy? I wrote about her in 1985, how we shared a great moment in history, V-E Day in London, the end of World War II in Europe. The war had about ended when my old 6th Armored Division finally halted deep in eastern Germany at Mittweida.

For reasons I never understood, I was only one of 20 other guys out of 10,000 to get a two-week furlough from the front. I chose to go to London because I learned to love the old city when we were stationed in England before the invasion.

I met Dorothy in a little photo shop at Piccadilly Circus. I had gone there to get my picture taken to send to my mother and dad to show them that I had emerged from the war unhurt. That brief meeting began a friendship that has endured for more than half a century.

What a time to be in London! The lights came on again after years of Luftwaffe night bombing. Dorothy and I saw the king and queen, and the future queen, Winston Churchill and millions of deliriously happy Londoners.

I spent my furlough in her parents' home. I gave Dorothy my little gold signet ring and she gave me a locket with her photo in it. When we parted at Waterloo Station, we both believed we would never see each other again.

The letters we promised became fewer and fewer and finally stopped. Forty years later, I am sitting at my desk in the newsroom. Joe Garner asked me if I had any memories of V-E Day. When I told him about Dorothy, he said, "You have to write that story."

I did. Of all the stuff I have cranked out for the *Rocky*, I think it was my best effort. Suzanne Weiss, who sat next to me then, said, "Geno, if someone had written a story about me like that, I would want to read it."

And that began what really was one of those six-degrees-of-separation stories. We finally found Dorothy living on a little farm in Tasmania, the island state of Australia.

We started corresponding again and telephoning each other every several months. Then Dorothy came to the United States to visit her son, who was working in New York. She stayed for a week with Trish and me in our home. It was a wonderful reunion. Joe came to the dinner party Trish had for her.

Her husband died, and now she is living in a senior-citizens home in West Tamar, Tasmania. Our phone calls have continued until now. Joe dropped me a note asking if I had talked to Dorothy yet about my entering hospice. I couldn't put it off any longer and called her.

I just came right out and told her I was dying, and I wanted to say goodbye. I don't need to explain what a tearful experience it was for both of us. The memories just flooded back about how young we were and how special our meeting was. The years melted away. She said she was thankful Trish was at my side and that I was getting hospice care. And then she said: "You know, Gene, I am so happy we lived in our time. Even with that terrible war, we had the best of years to live."

Indeed we did. Our adventure was incomparable. Dorothy said she will call again before Christmas.

November 28

Furor over beliefs just wasted energy

DUST.

Whose death is this, anyhow? Strike that. I'll have to admit that was my first reaction when so many readers wanted to tell me how to die. E-mail from everywhere was probably prompted by an interview I gave to Associated Press reporter Colleen Slevin.

I tried to be as honest with my answers as I could. I told her I don't believe in a heaven or hell in the hereafter if one really exists. I also said I had experienced bits and pieces of both heaven and hell in my 78 years of life.

Lately, I have been wondering what the big deal is. We are all going to die. It's just that I am going to have the experience sooner than most. All of us will eventually learn if our lives are eternal or not.

I am keeping this diary so others may be helped with many of the troubling and painful issues of getting ready to die. That's all. I am not trying to advance any religious belief or deny the validity of any other.

That's one of the things I like about hospice. It has no spiritual or religious agenda. Patients don't have to believe in any particular dogma. Agnostics and atheists can get hospice care as do Protestants, Catholics, Jews, Muslims or whatever. A chaplain is available if patients seek help with spiritual issues, but that is all.

My religious and/or spiritual beliefs are my own. They are private and personal and I am not seeking to impose them on anyone.

Having said that, I am grateful for well-intentioned readers who pray for me and are concerned about me as a friend, a person, or just an old guy who writes newspaper columns.

Not all are that well-intentioned, however.

Some are angry to the point of even being hateful. They threaten me with all manner of pain and agony in the afterlife if I don't subscribe to their fundamental beliefs.

Somehow, I can't bring myself to believe that a savior would save me by threatening me with violence.

Do I hate them?

Absolutely not. I gave up hating a long time ago.

Sure, I used to hate the Germans because of World War II. I hated them because I believed they were trying to kill me and because they robbed me of my youth.

Years ago, we had a young German exchange reporter working with us. I was so petty, I even refused to speak to him.

What a lot of foolish wasted energy that was. As I am getting ready to die there are some things I don't like, but my life is so short now I don't have time to hate anymore.

I thought I had better write this column because my beliefs, or lack of them, seem to be raising so much dust. Readers will just have to accept me the way I am. If they can't, so be it. Actually, that's always the way it has been with what I do here.

If I had my life to live over again, what would I change? Not much, I suspect. I have always tried to do the right thing as my parents taught me by their example. I loved them both, and they loved me.

In raising my children, I tried to be a positive influence on their lives as my parents had been on mine.

I needed no dogma for that.

November 29

Letter conjures up delightful memories

PITIFUL ATTEMPT.

Did you ever get a letter that opened a treasure of memories for you? I just did. It was from Betty Ray Thibodeau Modisett Ambler. It began: "Dammit—it shouldn't be like this. Was it Shaw who said (something like) 'Life's a pretty good play, with a poorly written third act'? Couldn't we just get better and better and better and fly away to some far place?"

If we could, I would want Betty to be there. I can close my eyes and still see her teaching the sixth grade at Bromwell Elementary School where my Muffy began her education.

The fun we have had over the years! I lived on East Seventh Avenue and she just off Seventh in a wondrous old Denver Square house that was always filled with surprises. Her husband had just died, leaving her to raise her son and daughter alone.

She wasn't one of those weepy widows, always playing the helpless game. She took life right by the horns and is still living it to the fullest.

Betty's son, Larry, was away at Williams College back East, and her daughter, Lani, was driving the boys crazy at East High.

That's where I came in. Somehow, things seemed to work out that I became a sort of temporary surrogate father for Lani. I hope she doesn't mind my writing that.

Anyhow, she kept wandering by and asking me to help with her homework. As I have written before, I was a wretched student, barely squeaking by in the bottom third of my high school class.

It didn't matter. We both sat down and tried to make sense of her English literature class. It was heavy going for this old guy, but once I got started, I loved it. We were picking apart the aforementioned George Bernard Shaw's *Man and Superman*, which was published in 1903.

Was it the fourth act we came to know as Don Juan in Hell? I think so. How I loved Shaw's language. Lani's homework and my pitiful attempt at helping her made Shaw my literary hero.

It wasn't just schoolwork. We all found ourselves having a lot of fun together, like going on mountain trips, that sort of thing. I tried to be there for Lani when she had romance problems or just needed a shoulder to cry on.

Those were wonderful times when we could all sit down at dinner and laugh at ourselves in Betty's old house. Nothing ever stays the same, though. Betty married Dr. John Ambler. Lani finished school, became a teacher, married and had children. We all saw each other just occasionally.

Time passed for me, too. I was divorced and remarried, and I became a father again for the fourth time when our daughter, Susan, was born. There were more memories to be unlocked when she went away to school in California.

Like Lani, Susan was having English literature problems, and I was trying to help her with a term paper over the telephone. Would you believe it was GBS again and *Man and Superman* again? True.

I bought the Cliff Notes and rediscovered the pleasures I thought I had misplaced all those years ago.

Thank you, Betty, thank you. If only we could all fly away to some far place.

Quote: "There is only one religion, though there are a hundred versions of it."—George Bernard Shaw.

November 30

Some days there's ramblin' on my mind

BULLWINKLE.

It's memory time again. These days are brimful of memories. Just the other morning I was fixing French toast and bacon for breakfast. Trish adores French toast, maybe even as much as apple fritters.

Sure, I'm still able to do some home cooking and enjoy doing it. When the bacon started to sizzle in the skillet, I thought of Cubby. His last name escapes me. He was one of the Deep River Boys who sang at the old Frontier nightclub on Colorado Boulevard where that strip joint used to be.

I did a stint as a stand-up emcee at the Frontier. A guy named Anderson owned it. I can't remember his first name. My memory is shot. Anyhow, he hired me as a stand-up emcee. It was an ambitious little club with a line of chorus girls and an eight-piece band.

That's where I met Max DiJulio. Both of us had just been discharged from the Army. Max had played with Gordon Dooley in the Glenn Miller Army Band. Henry Mancini was also in that band.

After the show at the Frontier every night, some of us would go out in the kitchen and Cubby would fry up a bunch of bacon and eggs. The bacon was just phenomenal. He said his secret was frying it slowly, over low heat.

I had always foolishly believed that you couldn't screw up bacon. But you don't want it rubbery, and you don't want it burned, either. Long after my Frontier days were over, I always took my time frying bacon because of Cubby's advice.

When Brett, Muffy and Jon were little, French toast or pancakes and bacon were a Saturday-morning ritual at our house. I can still see them sitting around the table waiting for the bacon to be ready. And if I imagine real hard, I can hear Rocky and Bullwinkle on that old black-and-white RCA television set I bought at a discount because I was working out of *The Denver Post*.

When Susan came along, I was back at the stove doing my French toast-and-bacon routine. Oh, yes, the bread is important. I used to think old Rainbow worked OK, but not anymore. French bread is for French toast, right?

Doug Miller came over the other night and did the nicest thing for Trish and me. He cooked up a mess of baby-back ribs and served them with a tossed green salad and a loaf of French bread and some eclairs from Child's bakery. Was that a neat thing for him to do or what?

Anyhow, there was enough bread left over for the French toast.

I like to splash some vanilla extract and milk in the beaten egg batter and then sprinkle the browned toast with powdered sugar when it's ready to serve.

I know I'm rambling some today, but this is my diary, isn't it? I just can't get over how nice people have been to our family now that my life is winding down. I wish there were some way I could personally respond to all the letters and messages I've been receiving, but I can't.

When the e-mails started coming, I tried to at least acknowledge them, but now I'm overwhelmed. I know that a blanket "thank you" isn't good enough, but it's the best I can do under the circumstances.

December 1

Memories of 17th Street call to me

Codicil.

I just got back from filling my eyes with 17th Street. I needed to do that before I die. The scurry and the hustle I loved are still there even if the old Denver banks and their fat-cat owners are gone.

It was my world, too, during my early radio years. I worked at a little station on the backside of the stately Equitable Building on Stout Street. Pop worked downtown, too, for a time in the old brownstone Boston Building. Sometimes we'd eat Swedish pancakes for lunch at Lund's over on 18th.

Do you care about this? Probably not. I don't mind telling you, though, I'm sorry there won't be a 17th Street for me to love anymore. The street will still be there, but I won't. As I write this, I am hearing "Moonlight in Vermont" played by Johnny Smith on his guitar at Shaner's.

I went downtown to sign a codicil on my will. Joyce Nakamura, my attorney, said she would come out to my house with a notary public to get my signature. I figured the ride downtown would do me some good, maybe my last time to see old 17th Street.

On the way down I thought about how lucky I am to have my death planned so well. Sounds crazy? My family will be in such a better place because Joyce, and my financial adviser, Jennifer Elmore, have helped me leave my house in order.

Supposing I just keeled over in my soup some night and left a big mess that would keep Trish's hands tied for months. I know that must happen all the time. It's not fair to the survivors. Anyhow, the paperwork took only a few minutes and we were on our way again.

Sure, I was pooped out, but I just loved being downtown again. I had seen Joyce and Jennifer just a couple of weeks ago when they came out to the house to help us sort through my will and things we wanted to do for our kids and little Jacob.

When we walked into Joyce's office she said I looked thinner. Others have said much the same thing, even my kids have noticed a change. Trish has mentioned it a couple of times.

She only explains that I am different. I don't know how. I still feel about the same, maybe a little weaker, though. I know I have been in a decline for some time now. Maybe I am slipping faster than I realize.

I still have hopes of getting everything done I had hoped to do. I'll just hang in here the best I can and hope for the best. You have noticed my columns are running almost every day now, not just three days a week.

That's OK by me. It would be nice if I could write everything I wanted to tell you while I still have the strength. But I guess it isn't my call to make. This is the first time in my life that I felt that I was no longer in control of what was happening to me.

It's something like I remember fighting in the war. I just didn't know then if I was going to make it. I didn't know if one of those terrifying 88 shells had Sgt. Amole's name on it.

Now is no time to worry. I think I'll just sit back until morning, close my eyes and remember Johnny Smith playing, "Pennies in a stream. Ski Trails down a mountainside. Moonlight in Vermont. Telegraph cables, how they sing down the highway. Moonlight in Vermont."

December 3

Lately, the old tunes keep playing in my head

SEAFOOD.

Maybe it is because I was a disc jockey for so long that I keep hearing old songs while I am getting ready to die. That's not exactly right. I don't actually hear them, but their melodies and lyrics linger in my memories. Just the other day I wrote that old 17th Street reminds me of Johnny Smith playing "Moonlight in Vermont" on his guitar at Shaner's Bar.

I hear another old song when I get out of the shower in the morning. My worst fear is that I'll slip, fall and break my hip. Very carefully, I grasp the grab bars I had installed in my shower some years back when I had a stroke. As I steady myself, reaching for a towel with one hand, while my other hand is on the grab bar, I find myself singing, "Hold Tight."

Remember the lyric the Andrews Sisters sang? "Hold tight. Hold Tight. Foodey Rackey Sackey. Want some sea food, Mama. Shrimpers and rice, they're very nice!"

OK, so that is a little loopy, but when I started this diary, I wanted to chronicle all the physical, mental and spiritual sensations I was experiencing. I seriously doubt they will prove useful to anyone, but they are playing a role in my dying process.

The song that just popped up on my imaginary juke box today was "Changes." Surely you must remember, "There'll be a change in the weather and a change in the scene, and pretty soon, baby, there'll be a change in me."

There is no doubt my body is changing. Even though I am eating better following the "roto-rooter" job on my throat, I have lost another pound. I am down to 129 now. I have also noticed my beard doesn't grow as fast as before, but my fingernails and toenails are growing faster.

The latter presents a problem for elderly people. You see, I don't mind being referred to as "elderly" the way so many old folks do. Hey, if you are elderly, you are elderly.

Anyhow, the toenail problem is exasperating whether you are getting ready to die or not. Toenails become thick, so thick they can't be trimmed with an ordinary over-the-counter toenail clipper. And if you have bad arthritis, it is almost impossible to lean over and trim them in the first place. Painful ingrown toenails can result if they aren't regularly clipped.

The solution: Go to a podiatrist, a doctor certified to treat foot ailments. It takes just a few minutes, and wow! What a relief! I go to Dr. Steven M. Atkins, associated with the Orthopedic Physicians of Colorado.

Older people should have their toenails clipped every four months.

Another change that's taking place in my body is my posture. I have always prided myself in standing straight, but now I am slumping over.

After all the neck and back surgery I have had, my height is no longer six feet. Until this latest setback in my health, I was 5-10, but now I suspect I am shorter than that.

I'm glad Trish keeps prompting me to stand up straight. I need that, but like all the rest of this exercise, it is a losing battle. But I'll keep trying.

In my mind I keep saying:

"A position of a soldier at attention. Head and eyes to the front. Arms hanging naturally from the shoulders. Backs of the hands out. Thumbs along the seams of the trousers. Knees straight without stiffness ... "

December 4

Harrison's passing can't kill memories

REVOLUTION.

At this writing, a generation is mourning the death of George Harrison. I thought *Denver Post* columnist Diane Carman had it exactly right when she wrote, "Sure, George's mortality reminds us of our own."

Obviously, I need no reminder of my mortality. It's just around the corner. His death, though, did remind me of the sweetness of the Baby Boomers I helped father. At the risk of repeating old anecdotes, something I find myself doing regularly, I am reminded of the night I took my daughter, Tustin, to hear the "Fab Four" at Red Rocks.

I hadn't intended to go. The deal was, if I bought the tickets, her mother would take her to the concert. It didn't work out that way, though. I had a tearful phone call from my daughter at two that afternoon.

"Daddy, Daddy," she cried, "Mom is sick and can't take me, and KIMN says the seats are all taken. Can you take me? Please! We have to leave right NOW!"

I dropped everything, and we joined the great procession to Red Rocks. As it turned out, the seats weren't all taken, and we found a pair almost smack-dab in the center of the arena.

I counted 40 police officers from every jurisdiction surrounding the stage. It was bedlam from start to finish. There was so much noise I couldn't hear the music. Neither could anyone else. It didn't matter. We had become a part of an event that would be repeated time and again everywhere the Beatles performed.

From my standpoint, though, there was one difference. Somehow, in all that earsplitting noise, I began to hear a small voice saying, over and over, "I love you, George. I love you."

Finally, I looked around and saw it was my 11-year-old daughter who loved George. I have no idea how many other little girls at Red Rocks that night also loved George Harrison, but I suspect there were many. Obviously, there still are.

Writers with much greater skill than I have written endlessly about the Beatles phenomenon. I finally came to the conclusion that my tired old generation was on the outside, looking in.

Now, the Boomers are finding out what it's like to be on the outside looking in. The Beatles were unique, though. In searching through my memories, I can't find anyone or anything as innovative or revolutionary in my generation as they were in theirs.

Old guys my age pretended to understand and be a part of that revolution, with their long hair, Nehru jackets and pukka necklaces, but I don't think they ever really got it. You had to be young and unspoiled by war and the Depression to really "get it."

Sure, we had our "Stardust," our cheek-to-cheek dancing, our rumble-seat fumbling, but nothing to equal the adoration that enveloped the Beatles. As Diane Carman, wrote, though, "George's death was a minor news event except that it forced us to face the reality of growing old ..."

The trick, of course, is to manage it gracefully. I have no advice. I am still trying to get the hang of it myself.

December 6

Eye-talia, I've had great pals

BAGELS.

It was good to hear from Larry Winograd, the man they call the Frontier Ophthalmologist. It's because his eye clinic is on the West Side. He calls it Villa Eye-talia.

Anyhow, Larry said he hoped I would be able to spit in the face of Malech Hamovas, Hebrew for Angel of Death. I am puckering and trying the best I can and still have some time left to enjoy old friendships.

Larry reminded me of our mutual friend, the late Dr. Ernie Forman, whose surgery practice was right next door to his Villa Eye-talia. When someone would die whom both knew, Larry would say, "Ernie, did you hear that so-and-so died?"

His standard reply was, "Yeah, people are dying today who have never died before."

Look, I'm not trying to take this trip I'm on too seriously. I have always needed a little humor to get through the day. Laughter has always been important to me and will continue to be, I hope, until my last breath.

I wish you could have known Ernie. It isn't much of a stretch for you to imagine him as a surgeon in a Korean War M*A*S*H unit, which he was. His parents owned Forman's Bakery on West Colfax. When he was a little boy, Ernie delivered fresh-baked bagels to Jewish families in the neighborhood.

The Jewish doctors and those of us who worked at little KDEN on Ruby Hill got acquainted at lunch at Berry's at South Federal and West Jewell. It is now Newbarry's but still owned by Spero Armatas, son of George Armatas, founder of Sam's #3 chili parlor. You can't leave out the Greeks. Boy, what a rich and wonderful life I have had! I wouldn't have wanted to miss any of these guys.

And that brings us to Ed Koepke, my business partner for more than 40 years. We met at little KMYR. He was a night engineer and I was the night announcer. He had been a patient at Lutheran Sanitarium, now Lutheran Medical Center.

Ed was recovering from tuberculosis. In those days, there were no medications to combat the disease. That's why so many people came to Colorado and its dry climate for treatment.

That's what brought us together, and what good fortune it was for me. He finally got out of engineering and into radio sales. I'll skip the details, but we had a chance to acquire a little radio station. Our partnership endured for all those years. We actually started with nothing. Zero.

We finally sold the last of our radio properties, KVOD, in 1983 because we were getting too old for what Pete Smythe called "the daily battle." Ed and I talked about this on the phone the other day and laughed that we never really had a plan.

We ran our business on what we believed to be our instincts to do the right thing. It was sad for us when we finally sold KVOD. We had become sort of extended family.

Because of Ed's poor health when we were young, he always said I would outlive him. He laughs and still thinks so. Not a chance, now. But that's OK. What a wonderful friend and partner he has been all these years. When our competitors in broadcasting talked about our success, they would often say, "Koepke had the brains and Amole had the mouth."

That's about right.

December 7

Let's hear it, folks, for effective writing

DOUBLE WHAMMY.

I was interested in Holly Yettick's piece in the *Rocky* about "Step Up to Writing," a new method of teaching children to write. It was developed by Maureen Auman, a former Cherry Creek middle school teacher.

As I understand its basis, "Step Up to Writing" is something like what we call a lead in journalism, with its beginning sentence summarizing the topic. The lead, as journalists have practiced it for years, strives to contain the who, what, where, when and why of a story.

The lead was developed because of a need to edit stories to fit available newspaper space. This meant copy editors could shorten stories from the bottom up without losing essential information packed in the top paragraphs.

I am not capable of evaluating Auman's "Step up to Writing" method because, I am embarrassed to admit, I never studied writing in school. I make the admission because some of my readers ask in their e-mail where and how I learned to write.

Now that I am getting ready to die, it is probably time to get this off my chest. When I look around the newsroom, I am the only one without a university education. I take no pride in this. I regret I never pursued higher education when I had the opportunity after I got out of the Army. My mother was a teacher, and she did teach me to respect the English language.

So, how did I learn to do what I do? You probably didn't notice, but I don't write for the eye, as writing has been taught for centuries. I write for the ear. I don't want my readers to "see" my words. I want them to "hear" my words.

Learning to write this way was an evolutionary process for me because my career in journalism began in radio. When I wrote a news story, I wrote it to be comfortable in my mouth.

When I started in this business, there were two main wire news services, The Associated Press and United Press. Both transmitted their copy mainly to newspapers. It was written for the eye.

When radio news became competitive, United Press discovered it could get more clients by offering a separate service tailoring its copy to be read over the air, not seen in a newspaper. It wasn't long before The Associated Press followed suit with its broadcast wire.

I don't have sufficient space here to illustrate the differences between broadcast and newspaper copy. I like to think my column can be read aloud comfortably. This isn't always the case with stories written for newspapers.

Years ago I wrote a television documentary about Evans School. It was a Denver public elementary school in a blue-collar district. It differed from other schools because blind and deaf children from all over the district were educated there, too. The idea was to mainstream them as quickly as possible.

I was surprised to learn that blind children could be mainstreamed faster than deaf children. I would have thought the reverse would have been true. Not so. Teachers at Evans found that so much of what children were learning was through hearing, not seeing.

It is my own theory that if written material can be "heard" as well as "seen," its meaning will be reinforced because of this "double-whammy" factor.

I doubt, though, that my half-baked theory will ever find its way into teaching kids to write.

December 8

Struggle is to keep awake for readers

Awake.

If I had to pinpoint a time and place where my dying process began, I would have to say it was last year on South Sheridan Boulevard and U.S. 285. I had a seizure while driving home from work and smacked into a guy driving a red Mercedes-Benz.

I felt awful about it. The cops and fire department guys were very kind. My little Jeep Cherokee couldn't be driven. The tow-truck driver was kind enough to take me home.

That incident ended my driving any kind of car, even my cherished Stingray Corvette.

The seizure was probably a throwback from a stroke I had suffered some years back. I kept having little blackouts at work and when driving home when I was tired. I tried several kinds of medications but none worked.

The truth is that I shouldn't have been driving at all. It's a very difficult decision for old people to quit driving. If you can't drive in this town, you are pretty well isolated. I continued to work, though, as I am now. While I was still able to work in the newsroom, Trish and my sons taxied me back and forth.

I am still having the seizures, only they are more frequent. Maybe seizure isn't the right word. I just nod off, involuntarily, even while eating or just talking on the telephone.

I even nod off while writing this column. I ask myself this embarrassing question: "If I can't keep myself awake, how can I ever hope to keep my readers awake?" I struggle with this all the time.

I avoid taking pain medication because I am afraid I won't be able to think clearly. Same thing with typing. Normally, I am a fast typist, but there are times when my fingers won't obey my brain and I am reduced to hunting and pecking.

Some people can get by with that. Bill Gallo, one of the best newspaper writers I have ever known, sat next to me for a time in the newsroom.

He hammered relentlessly at the keyboard with just his forefingers. His copy was perfect.

I guess I hate it that I am losing what skills I once had. Now, I have to write, rewrite, rewrite and rewrite some more. It never seems right to me.

Of what I do, I have always said that when I file my copy, it is the best I can do on that given day, and sometimes it isn't good enough.

There is something else that is most likely a part of the dying process. I am having an increasing number of little dizzy spells. I thought maybe it was because I wasn't getting enough to eat, but now I am since I had the roto-rooter procedure done on my throat.

Add to all this the confusion I sometimes feel and maybe you are getting the picture of how I feel getting ready to die. Confusion is probably something most old people experience to some degree.

Sometimes I can't retain for even a few minutes conversations I have had with Trish. I have to laugh at myself, though. I can see old movies again and think I am seeing them for the first time. Sure saves on the pay-for-view bill.

You get the drill.

December 10

Yep. The blues can get to be part of the deal

MACABRE.

Sure, I get the blues. This dying business is not all beer and skittles. Mornings are rough. The pain in my legs awakens me to the reality that I am still alive and facing another day of waiting to die.

Of course everyone is waiting to die, but when you are coming smack dab against it, your attitude changes. Some mornings I find myself wishing death would come today, right now. I want to get it over with.

Then, I ask myself, why? Death isn't a worrisome task to be done with so I can get on with something else. The blues don't last all day. As soon as I shower, brush my teeth and splash on a little Mennen's after-shave, I feel better.

Trish tries to get me to slow down. I guess I am just not built that way, though. I feel better when I am doing something, like picking up the dishes and scrubbing pots and pans after dinner. When that is done,

I look around to see what else I am able to do. Of course my weakness limits what I can do, but I keep trying.

Writing this column helps me. Maybe it is some kind of therapy to empty my thoughts through my fingers.

The cards and letters I receive help a great deal, too. Sometimes I get a little smile, like the card I received from Floyd H. Keener, up in Loveland. It's in the shape of an orange.

It says, "I look at the navel of a navel orange, and I think, 'That looks nothing like my navel.' Then I put a little lint in it, and I think, 'Well, OK, it kind of does.'"

I also got a chuckle from a letter I wasn't supposed to receive. It was somehow mixed in with hundreds of letters addressed to me. This one was addressed to John Temple, editor, publisher and president of the *Rocky Mountain News*.

It was from Miller Hudson, a former Colorado legislator, lobbyist and all-around public policy gadfly. Miller wasn't extending his condolences, though. He wants my job.

Yes. He writes, "I realize it is a little macabre to be discussing Gene Amole's slot in the paper while he is still writing, but I've had a long-standing interest in applying for his position when or if it were to open."

To some it would seem "macabre" not to wait until my body is cold, but it is clear that Hudson wants to be the early bird who gets the worm. He who hesitates is lost, so to speak.

Hudson writes that he has several sample columns he would like Temple to read. Not wanting to appear overly insensitive to my situation, he closes his letter with: "This is likely not the appropriate time for such a discussion, but I hope you will file this letter away for later consideration. In the meantime, let me wish you and yours a happy holiday season."

Ho! Ho!

On the subject of my mail, I want to express my gratitude to Michelle Quintana who has somehow found time to deal with the torrent of mail I have received since I have become a hospice patient.

She is regularly John Temple's secretary, a demanding job itself. Where and when does she find time to be my personal secretary, too? I don't know because I can't get into the newsroom to find out. I just want her to know, though, how much my family and I appreciate what she is doing for us.

Old oak buffet stays; snow shovel goes

AUNT MINNIE.

Often, when I start to add a page to my diary, I don't have a clue of what I am going to write. I just hook up my brain to my fingers to see what happens. Sometimes I get to thinking about stuff I won't have to do anymore.

There is no question about it, I am through with snow shoveling. This is the first winter in my memory that someone else will have to clear my sidewalks and driveway.

I have had lung problems for some time, and the last three years I have had to rig up a portable oxygen tank on my back to push the snow-blower. I looked pretty funny. My lungs probably suffered further damage because the fumes from the two-cycle motor were pretty rancid.

I wonder if anyone has done a study on toxic fumes inhaled from snow blowers. I knew they certainly weren't helping my lungs, clogged as they are with irreversible pulmonary fibrosis. But I thought, "What the hell, I'll hurry up and avoid further damage, and this sure beats pushing a shovel."

You see how the mind works? We can always find excuses for not doing the right thing. My heart was always in the right place, though. My mom was 86 when she died. For years when it snowed, I would drive over to her house early in the morning to clean her walks.

I would have to hurry, though. Sometimes she would call me and tell me not to come because she had already shoveled her walks. Imagine that, 86 and still cleaning her own walks. Our old house is on a corner, too, and has plenty of walks to shovel. My son, Brett, lives there now, and it's his responsibility.

My great-grandfather, Billy Fiedler, built that house more than 100 years ago and the duplex next door and also the old place at 22nd and Newton where Aunt Minnie lived. He also built other houses and a few churches in north Denver, but we never kept track of where they are. Should have.

Grandpa Fiedler didn't call himself a carpenter, but a "builder." I like that. I always wanted to have those skills, to be a builder. It was no go. Couldn't even hammer a nail straight.

Old guys in his day bartered their skills. We have a wonderful old oak buffet in our house. It has beveled mirrors and solid brass pulls. I love the floral carving on the doors. Grandpa helped a friend build his farmhouse back in Iowa before he came west to Colorado.

The friend was a cabinet maker, and instead of paying Grandpa, he gave him the buffet. Grandma Lizzie wouldn't hear of leaving it back in Iowa when they came west. For years it was on the back porch of our old house. Mom kept her gardening tools in it. She told me she was tired of it taking up so much space and would call Goodwill to haul it away.

I rescued it and have had it restored a couple of times. It's beautiful. I love it, but I'll be leaving it behind. Trish will take good care of it, though. Someday maybe little Jacob's family will inherit it.

By the way, I am leaving Grandpa Amole's Illinois railroad pocket watch and my dad's gold pocket watch to Jacob. They are both more than 100 years old, and its very important to me that they stay in our family. I know Jacob will appreciate them and care for them when he is old enough.

December 12

Readers recall my golden radio days

DARKNESS.

If there was only a way I could personally thank each person who has been kind enough to write to me, I would certainly do it. There are just too many, though—so many I haven't been able to count them. Reading them is a humbling experience.

I sit up and read and read until my back hurts so much I have to lie down. If there is such a thing as pleasant pain, this must be it. Most letters are very flattering. Some are amusing, like the number of "get-well" cards I am receiving.

Even though this diary results from my newspaper column, a surprising number of letters are about my radio days. Geez, I haven't been on the radio since 1983. When I started in radio broadcasting more than a half-century ago, I loved the mystery of it.

There was no television then, just voices, music and other invisible sounds that came to us through the air. I thought it was a miracle then, and I still think it is now. As a child, I listened to the radio on a crystal set Grandpa Amole rigged up in the dining room of our house at 64 W. Maple Ave.

He'd fiddle with the thing until he heard something on his earphones. Then he'd clasp the phones in his big calloused hands over my ears. "It's Cincinnati, Bub," he would say. "It's Cincinnati!"

Then we got the local stations. First, it was Doc Reynolds' KLZ, "The pioneer broadcast station of the West," the announcer would say. I was hooked. I listened to Uncle Gene and Holly on KFEL and The Men of the West on KOA.

I wanted to be one of those guys who baritoned their way over the ether. I finally got my break in 1941, just as World War II broke out, on little KMYR, and came back to work there after I got out of the Army.

There is no space here to describe all my radio adventures, but I am so pleased that many readers wrote to me about what they remembered. So many memories were about KVOD and the years I spent hosting Music for a New Day.

They wrote about the birds I fed outside the studio window and my Friday waltz fantasies from imaginary Chateau Ruby Hill. They remembered the annual Denver Symphony Orchestra Marathon broadcasts we did from the May Co. window on 16th Street, and the Beethoven birthday parties.

Even earlier than that, readers remembered the fun Lloyd Knight and I had on little KDEN, the first radio station Ed Koepke and I owned. Let me tell you this, no funnier man ever spoke into a microphone than Lloyd Knight. It was really my show, but I became his straight man.

It has been many years since he took his own life. In notes he left for me and others, he considered himself a failure. For 40 years, folks have not forgotten him. He was a failure only in his own mind, not to others. People who are considering suicide as an answer to their problems ought to remember Lloyd Knight before they pull the trigger.

Oh, those wonderful radio days. They made my life worth living, and thanks to all of you who remember their magic as I do. I can still close my eyes when I am alone and hear Wes Battersea say on KLZ, "Little old world, good afternoon!"

And that music in the background, is it Milt Shrednik's orchestra on KOA? And is it time to tune in to The Air Adventures of Jimmy Allen? And One Man's Family, is it still out there, somewhere in the darkness?

December 13

I can't take it with me? Say it ain't so

CODGER.

An aging ophthalmologist of my acquaintance wants me to find out whether there's sex after death. I told him a more appropriate question for me is: Are there dark chocolate-covered Dove vanilla ice cream bars after death?

If there were only a way I could take some with me. Some readers might suggest that they would melt instantly. Not all share that view, however. You may recall a diary page in which Sister Mary Louise Beutner spoke to me about my disbelief in an afterlife.

"Boy, do you have a nice surprise waiting for you," she said with an impish grin.

I've just received a letter from another Loretto nun. Sister Katherine Ann Heinz writes: "I can just see our Sister Mary Louise standing behind St. Peter when you show up, saying, 'Pete, let the old codger in, he is really quite harmless.' You will make heaven a more interesting place, I am sure."

All this reminds me of a nice little movie Trish and I watched on pay-per-view the other night. It was Chocolat, the story of a young unmarried mother of a little girl who moves to a small French town.

The mother was a chocolatier, or a maker of fine chocolate products. She angered the pious mayor of the town by opening a shop on the first day of Lent. He enlists the parish priest in a campaign to run her out of town.

In the end, he fails and winds up gorging himself with chocolate in the window of her shop.

I don't know how often chocolate has been linked with sin. If there is any truth to that, I'm destined to be melted along with the Dove bars.

"Not to worry," Trish says. "You eat dark chocolate. It's milk chocolate that's bad for your health."

It must be something in the genes. My whole family goes bonkers over chocolate.

Do you suppose it's a sin for Trish and me to drink Cafe Godiva chocolate Arabica coffee avec creme brulee on Sunday mornings?

Whether we'll be able to miss anything or anyone after we die remains an open question for all of us. Certainly, Dove bars would be near the top on my list if we do. Foolishly, I suppose, I think often of what I'll miss by not being alive. Fried chicken ranks way up there, too, along with pot roast and baby-back ribs.

I'm still able to cook some, and the other night I simmered up a pot of corned beef and cabbage. It's a good two-or-three-day meal. I like to slice the brisket paper-thin the next day and make it into Reuben sandwiches.

You alternate layers of corned beef, Dijon mustard, Ed McCaffrey horseradish, Swiss cheese and sauerkraut between slices of dark Jewish pumpernickel and then grill them on both sides in a hot skillet.

If there's any corned beef left the third day, grind it in a food processor and combine with peeled and boiled potatoes cut in small cubes, a finely processed white onion, Worcestershire sauce, salt and pepper and about a half-cup of milk.

Then, of course, you brown it in a hot, greased skillet. Serve as is, but if you want to be fancy, place a poached egg on each serving.

Yeah, you're right about that—I'll miss corned beef hash, too.

December 14

I'm humbled by those who paved the way

INFINITIVE.

What can I say? What can I possibly say about the name of Elati Street, across from the *Rocky Mountain News*, being changed to Gene Amole Way? And on top of that, the address of Denver's favorite newspaper will be changed from 400 West Colfax Ave. to 100 Gene Amole Way.

Let me put it this way: How would you feel? Well, you don't know because it hasn't happened to you. It has happened to me, and I am overwhelmed. When Lisa Levitt Ryckman called Wednesday night to tell me about the honor for a story she was writing, I just didn't know what to say.

Of course I am humbled by this recognition. My first thoughts were about those who deserved the honor much more than I. I thought of Jack Foster, who saved this newspaper from extinction back in the 1940s. Lee Taylor Casey, certainly, for the thousands of columns he wrote while recovering in Denver from tuberculosis.

And then there was Gene Cervi, the "stormy petrel" of Democratic Party politics before he published his own weekly newspaper. How about Molly Mayfield, whose saucy advice to the lovelorn column amused *Rocky* readers during and after World War II? Bob Perkin's name belongs up there for his First Hundred Years history of this newspaper. And what about Pocky Marranzino and Bob Chase and Vince Dwyer?

There are others who deserve the honor, folks whose names you never see, back shop people who put this newspaper together every day, pressmen who print it, classified ad salespeople, clerks, reporters, the people who deliver the paper and so many more.

And so to be selected from all of those past and present *Rocky Mountain News* employees is a great honor, and I am humbled by it.

I am indebted to Mayor Wellington Webb who made this possible. Aside from politics, I have always considered him a friend. Don't you choose people to be your friends because you like them personally?

I have always liked the mayor. I am comfortable around him. We both have Denver in our bones. We speak the same language. I so enjoyed lunch with him a couple of years ago in Five Points at the Kapre Fried Chicken restaurant where they also do justice to ribs and catfish.

The mayor attended Manual High when Jim Ward was principal, one of the top educators this town has ever seen, and also when Genevieve Lindemann taught English there. Man, you had better not split an infinitive around that lady.

My father attended Manual High, Manual Training High in those days. That's when Manual's sports teams were known as the Bricklayers.

Speaking of my father, Mayor Webb couldn't have known this, but Gene Amole Way is only a block from where my father, Frank Amole, was born. Kids were born at home in those days, and home was not far from the railroad where Grandpa worked.

Of course I am pleased by this recognition as is our family. I am happy for my grandson, Jacob, who will be able to show his friends Gene Amole Way and tell them that's where his grandpa worked.

December 15

Martha Stewart a very busy body

CHIANTI.

I have been taking time out of my busy day to consider Martha Stewart's calendar. Of course I'm busy. Do you think I am just lying around here waiting for the grim reaper?

Let me tell you something: Martha Stewart is one busy lady. She prints her monthly calendar in her magazine *Martha Stewart Living*, which is certainly more interesting than Gene Amole Dying. As I write this, for example, she is celebrating Chip Gibson's birthday and is getting her ornaments from the attic.

Yesterday morning at 8:36 Martha was appearing on the CBS *The Early Show* and took time out to celebrate Susan Magrino's birthday. Martha is very big on birthdays. She is celebrating at least six in December alone.

It's been a busy month for her. On Dec. 2, she practiced yoga in the morning and wrote or e-mailed her Christmas cards. The next day she continued wrapping hedge bottoms and sides with burlap. Then she put up her outdoor wreaths.

I guess I must have missed it, but on Dec. 4 she appeared on "Home for the Holidays" on CBS and then she sprayed her roses and evergreens with deer repellent. Gotta keep those deer outta the back yard.

On Dec. 6, she celebrated Rita Christiansen's birthday and spoke before the Japan Society in New York. Domo arigato, Martha! The next day she didn't observe Pearl Harbor Day, though, but had her ice skates sharpened and her cross-country skis tuned.

Dec. 9 was busy for Martha. She celebrated the first night of Hanukkah after yoga in the morning and baking cookies in the afternoon. The 10th was really a biggie for her. Martha baked gingerbread and assembled her gingerbread house. And if that wasn't enough, the poor dear had to prune her fruit trees.

The next day, Martha spent a good part of it cleaning the chandeliers and packing cookies for gifts. Jumping ahead, Martha will celebrate Jane Heller's birthday on Sunday, practice yoga in the morning and trim the tree.

Monday is an easy day for her. All she has to do is order a crown pork roast for Christmas. The next day, she will take time out from celebrating Kevin Sharkey's birthday to order rose bushes for spring delivery.

The next morning, Martha is on CBS again and celebrates Doug Brenner's birthday. She'll make gravlax the next day and will finish wrapping presents. The dogs go to the groomer the next day, and Martha will take time to prune espaliers.

The 22nd sounds like an ugly day to me. She is going to bathe her cats and then will hang the mistletoe. Martha seems to be winding down on the 23rd. Just yoga in the morning and a hike in the afternoon.

Christmas Eve, she'll assemble the croquembouche. Sure as hell gotta get the croquembouche assembled and then set the holiday table. Christmas Day is Larry Kennedy's birthday and Martha has to decorate her dogs. Who let the dogs out?

This reminds me of another Martha, Martha Scott, the English author. She said: "Do not make the mistake of treating your dogs like humans or they will treat you like dogs."

We're not as fancy as Martha Stewart at our house. Last night, we opened our presents early, after some pizza and Paisano chianti. It was great to see Jacob.

December 17

Look at your own life and cut Issel some slack

GOOD WORKS.

Enough, already. It's time to cut Dan Issel some slack.

Of course it was a terrible thing he shouted at that Pepsi Center fan. Sure, his ethnic slur hurt his team, Nuggets fans and his family. No one denies this, not even Dan Issel.

If you watched him almost sob out his apology on television, you know the person he hurt the most was himself. So, beyond his suspension, his fine and his public humiliation, just how much more punishment does he deserve?

When I saw that photo of Issel in the *Rocky Mountain News* above that story of how I am being honored with a street named after me, I felt guilt surge through my body. Many years ago, I was provoked into saying something not unlike that which is causing him so much grief.

I regretted it the instant I said it, but my regret came too late to prevent those I assailed from being harmed. What happens to us when we let our anger take command of our senses?

I don't know, but I suspect there is a dark side to all of us. None of us is perfect. When we rise up in righteous indignation over someone else's bad judgment, we are usually denying our own.

In Issel's case, he gets hammered again and again because he is a celebrity. Society loves to clobber celebrities because we mistakenly believe that by toppling them, we empower ourselves. Nonsense.

Now that I am dying, I am doing a lot of reflecting on my life. Let me be honest about this: There is some of it I would just as soon forget. I think to myself, "My God, why did I ever do that?"

Everyday, I sit down before an unbelievable amount of e-mail and snail-mail messages. Almost all of it is complimentary. Naturally, I am pleased that my work in radio, television and in this newspaper has met with so much popular approval.

This is tempered by my understanding that those who don't approve of me aren't sending messages at all, are not telling me, "I'll be glad when you're dead, you rascal, you," as the old song says.

Still, as you have seen in my columns, I do give my detractors a free shot at me now and then. Some will write again and apologize for what they said earlier. Those who don't probably get some satisfaction from telling me in print what a boob I am.

I don't know Dan Issel. I met him only once. It was at a luncheon where he was honored, I kid you not, by Hospice of Metro Denver for his good works in the community. This was before he coached the Nuggets and while he was still a player.

He found time then to help the community where he lived, raise his family and work. That should be worth something if we are going to examine the worth of him in our world.

In much of the mail I have received, readers have admonished me to read certain passages from the Bible. Most of them do so in my best interest, caring that I shall find a measure of peace in the afterlife.

In that same spirit, may I offer one of my favorite passages that seems appropriate now that everyone is coming down so hard on Dan Issel.

It is John 8.7: "He that is without sin among you, let him first cast a stone at her."

December 19

Very blessed am I and ready to die

DETACHED.

My hospice nurse says I have tissue-paper skin. There is a medical term for it, but I can't remember it. My skin appears very thin, almost transparent. I have lots of splotchy, purple bruises.

These are caused by two medications I am taking, prednisone and coumadin.

The prednisone is for pain, and the coumadin prevents blood clots from forming that might cause a stroke.

These marks appear mostly on my hands and arms and not on my face. They do not cause any pain. I mention this because my skin condition is one of the signs that I am dying.

Trish and I had a long talk with my hospice nurse about how and when I might die. We need as much information as we can get so it will help us plan to use the time I have left.

Will I be able to die at home, or will I have to spend the rest of my last days in the Hospice of Metro Denver residence facility? Of course I want to die in my own bed in our own home.

If my care becomes too difficult for Trish to manage here, I would want to die at the residence facility. I have seen it, and it is very pleasant and well-staffed with caring professionals.

It isn't likely I shall have an "event," a term used to define death as the result of a stroke, massive heart attack, or some other sudden happening.

It appears now that I will gradually surrender my life as a result of what is called a multisystem failure. That means my vital organs will no longer be able to sustain my life.

This process is already under way. One sign this is happening is I am gradually becoming "detached," as my hospice nurse describes my condition.

This means I am sleeping a lot. As I noted in this diary before, I actually nod off while writing entries in it, or go to sleep while reading a newspaper, or talking to friends on the telephone. I just drift away.

I try not to be detached completely from reality. I still want to know what is happening around me. I want to see my Trish, my sons and daughters, my son-in-law and my precious little Jacob. I want to cling to those I love as long as I can.

I think I shall be able to enjoy Christmas with them, but how much time after that, I don't know. At this point, I feel fortunate that my passing has been as pain- and anguish-free as it has.

I have Trish, my caregiver, and drugs to make this possible. It is so sad that for many years the medical profession was not schooled in helping their patients die comfortably, and doctors hesitated too long in prescribing pain medication.

They are rarely present when a patient dies. They are not there to ease the pain, to offer emotional as well as palliative support during the last days of life. It is more often the nurses who have had to assume these roles.

It is because of them that the hospice program has evolved.

Some medical schools are beginning to include training in their curriculum to help physicians be more responsive to their dying patients' needs.

As for me, I am grateful for the care my family and hospice have given me. They have made it possible for me to reflect on my life in the most positive terms. I have no anger, no hate, no fear. I am blessed, and I am ready to die.

December 20

It's nice to know old friends don't forget

ELEGANTLY.

One of the nice things about dying is that you hear from old friends you thought had forgotten you.

Ross Mark. It was sometime in the 1950s and I was pretending to be a war correspondent in Korea. You may recall the war was yo-yoing up and down the Korean peninsula. North Korea had invaded South Korea, and President Harry Truman mustered a United Nations force to throw the rascals back.

I was in Switzerland when it started. I thought I had to go to Korea to tell the story of the poor devils who were actually fighting the war. My experience as a soldier in World War II left me with serious doubts that the press would or could actually do this.

As it turned out, I was no better at it than those who preceded me. There must have been 200 or 300 of us trying to write those stories. I suppose we told ourselves we were there for the noblest of reasons. Actually, some of us were there to drink too much, to throw ourselves headlong into brawls at Myoshi's geisha house on Tokyo's Ginza, to play poker with the Brits and to compose off-color doggerel about Madam Chiang Kai-shek.

Ross Mark was a correspondent for the Australian Associated Press. We became friends. He let me tag along after him in hopes I could learn to put one word after another as elegantly as he.

We separated about the time the Panmunjom peace conference began, only to be reunited 50 years later in the U.S. mail by attorney Richard M. Schmidt Jr., general counsel for the American Society of Newspaper Editors and Publishers.

You see, I know a few big shots, too.

By chance, Ross and Dick are neighbors in Washington. Ross sent me a letter concerning my decision to vacate the planet in the public interest.

Let me tell you something—the old boy still knows how to write.

Pat Larkin. Readers may recall my sad tale of seeking her affection while AP correspondent Richard Kilroy O'Malley was trying to do the same thing. You may also remember that she would have neither of us because of our unsightly appearance in the lot where she parked her car next to the Arcade Pool Hall on Welton Street.

Our loss was certainly her gain. She tunneled out of the journalism game, married, became a mother and a grandmother and lived happily ever after. She, too, was skilled at putting one word after another: "You already know I'm thinking of you," she writes. "Someday, in some small dim cafe, the willow will weep for you. And I pray your agenda will include at least a million smiles. Love to you and Trish."

Jim Strain, M.D. We have been friends since we were in the fourth grade at Steele School. Sure, he became a nationally respected and honored pediatrician, but he wasn't too busy to take care of my kids, Tustin, Brett, Jon and Susan "at my office at 6th and Josephine and later at Leetsdale and Jersey," he writes. "I enjoyed so much visiting with Patricia, who always impressed me as a very loving and capable mother."

Jimmy says I am the reason he has subscribed to the *Rocky* even though he remained loyal to *The Denver Post* because his father, Elmer Strain, was director of national advertising for the *Post* for more than 40 years.

Hey, Jimmy, does this mean you are going to cancel when I check out?

December 21
Saying goodbye overwhelming

OVERWHELMED.

Usually, when I sit down to write a column, I just put my fingers on the keyboard, and they will know what to do. Not today.

Trish and I just returned home from my first visit to the *Rocky Mountain News* in many months. After I decided to write my diary about dying, I didn't think I could handle going back there again.

There were just too many memories, too many people I respected and admired that I just didn't want to say goodbye to them and to our great old newspaper. I was afraid I would cry.

I did. I was overwhelmed.

It was such a cold day. I couldn't believe so many people would come downtown to watch Elati Street between West Colfax Avenue and West 14th Avenue be renamed Gene Amole Way, but they did. I wish I could somehow thank each one personally, but this will have to do.

Feelings don't always come out the way you want them to in print. I mean, how do you describe how your breath comes up short when you are trying to say something you hope folks will remember?

You will have to try to imagine how pleased I was to see so many of my newsroom pals out there in the cold, too. I remembered 1977 when I wrote my first column for the *Rocky*, and how scared I was the reporters wouldn't approve of me.

There were some friendly *Denver Post* faces out there in the crowd and some old friends from the TV stations, too. Channel 4's Larry Green ambushed me with a microphone.

I have not decided yet whether, or if, I am going to do any TV interviews about my column. All along, I have thought of this diary as something personal between my readers and me. They are the ones with whom I have a relationship.

What a friend Dusty Saunders has been through the years. I have known him since he was a young reporter on the cop beat. Let me tell you something about him: Dusty has written more and better newspaper copy than anyone in this nation. Period. He is incomparable. I was honored he was chosen to be master of ceremonies.

I was also pleased John Temple, my boss, my leader and my friend brought his family to the ceremony, too. This town became the richer for his decision to move to Denver and ultimately to become our top guy. He's here to stay.

None of this would have been possible without Mayor Wellington Webb. He did it, I am sure, because of our friendship. As we both would agree, we have never let minor disagreements interfere with that friendship.

I did the best I could walking through the crowd, trying to speak to people, to shake hands with them, to exchange a few words, but I wasn't very good at it because of my oxygen tank.

Trish and I were pleased all of our kids were there, and we were so proud of Jacob, our grandson, and how he sat there next to me with his hands folded in his lap. I am sure someone must have taken a picture of us that way.

Again, I wish my fingers could have done a better job for me today.

December 22

No man's an island, even while dying

INWARD.

If you're not careful, this dying business can be egocentric. I have noticed it's happening to me. Everything is about me, me, me. Sure, I'm the one who is doing the dying, and I have lapsed into thinking I am the only one involved. Wrong.

In chatting with Andrea VanSteenhouse the other day, the subject of detachment came up. She spoke of losing a loved one and how difficult it was for her that the person seemed to be pulling away from her as death approached.

You'll have to excuse my forgetfulness, but it seems to me I wrote a column about how the dying person gradually turns inward as death approaches. I can feel this happening to me now.

A part of what I am attempting to do with this diary is explain what it feels like to die. There are a lot of obvious things, like regret, fear, remorse, sorrow, anxiety, envy of those who will live on, stuff like that.

I have to say that, so far, I have not been afraid. People often ask me about this, reflecting, I suppose, their own fear of death. Maybe there is some kind of process I don't understand that is protecting me from fear.

Maybe it was my combat service in World War II that insulated me from fear of death. I don't know.

Getting back to egocentrism, if that's what it is, there has been a tendency on my part not to consider the feelings of others, particularly Trish. Unconsciously, I am probably saying to myself, "Look, Geno, I am the one who is dying around here, and I deserve all the consideration."

Damn, as I write this, I realize how selfish that is. I haven't been living in a cocoon. My life doesn't exist by itself. It is woven into the fabric of our family. As I grow weaker and less able to care for myself, the fabric loses some of its strength. What I have to do is keep reminding myself that I am not dying alone, that part of my family is dying with me.

While I am turning inward, I must also be conscious of my responsibility to Trish and the other members of my family. It would be wrong to shut them out of the process. They are all a part of me.

There are daily reminders I am dying. For example, I never seem to be able to stay warm. My daughter, Tustin, noticed this and bought me a little space heater for under the desk where I am writing this. Little things like that mean a lot.

I have also noticed I am getting a tingling sensation in my scalp. It sort of comes and goes. The thumb of my right hand turns numb occasionally from the knuckle up to the fingernail. I don't know what that's all about.

Probably nothing. I worry, though, that if I lose my ability to type, I'll be out of business.

I would sure be out of business if my son, Jon, wasn't a computer technician. He has kept my outdated equipment up and running. Same thing with my broken-down television stuff. I can't stop wondering what old dying guys do without caregivers like I have. Do they just curl up in the corner and die alone?

My hospice nurse tells me that as death approaches, my ability to write this diary will decline until I finally will stop. Hasn't happened yet. I don't know how much longer I can carry on, though.

I'll just keep cranking them out.

December 24

How many desk drawers hold dreams that never came true?

WASHED UP.

Is it natural to wonder what you have missed when you are about to die? That thought passed through my mind the other night as I watched a documentary on the Bravo arts TV channel. It was about Graham Greene's autobiographical novel, *The End of the Affair*.

The book was made into a film, and the documentary used it to show parallels between Greene's life and his novel. It was about a romantic affair he had with the wife of one of his best friends.

As I watched the program, I thought to myself, "My God, nothing like that ever happened to me, and thank God it didn't." I don't know how he ever managed it, considering that he was a Roman Catholic convert. Maybe in his mind he thought of the novel as a confession.

No matter. The reason I thought of myself in this context was that compared to him, I have led a pretty pedestrian life. Writing is what I do for a living, but I don't think of myself as a writer as he was.

I wanted to be once. I took a two-month leave of absence from the *Rocky* some years back to write a novel. It was about a washed-up newspaper columnist who was married to a hotshot investment banker. Sharp with money but cold as ice.

He was operating a one-man public relations company that specialized in political strategy. The poor jerk let himself be talked into forming a new advertising and public relations agency with a coke-sniffing huckster who was behind in his Porsche car payments.

A Southern Baptist preacher entered the scene with a plan to build a senior citizens community he would name "Maturity Manor." He was a real piece of work, this guy. He started all his meetings by having his salesmen join hands in prayer.

His plan was to collect upfront money from well-heeled seniors to build the kind of upscale retirement homes they wanted. "We want nice little people," he would say. "We don't want any of those old folks who are droolin' on their ties and are forgettin' to zip up their pants." I actually knew a guy like this.

Maturity Manor was the first big advertising account the new partnership had, and it laid out big money for an advertising campaign. The problem was, the preacher disappeared with the upfront money, leaving the huckster and the burned-out flack holding the bag.

The investment banker dumped the flack because of the bad Maturity Manor publicity. The coke snorter's Porsche was repossessed, and the burned-out flack fell into the arms of an overage ski bunny who had just abandoned Aspen in her banged-up Toyota.

Is this making you sick? It is me. I cranked out about five chapters of this trash and left it in the hard drive of my first Radio Shack computer. I did make a dot matrix hard copy, though, and kept it in the bottom drawer of my desk at home.

In cleaning up my papers and getting ready to die, I found the hard copy the other day. I threw it in the Waste Management trash barrel, which was a kinder fate than it deserved.

The title of the book? *Cottonwood*, because the flack and the ski bunny finally found a measure of happiness in a cheap trailer court under the cottonwoods near the old horse track. I have always had a special feeling for cottonwood trees.

Christmas treat at Amoles: Brunch

Ho! Ho!

I am ho ho-ing because I lived long enough to enjoy this day with my family. This will surely be my last Christmas, and it is just the way I wanted it. We are all together at our house right now enjoying our traditional Christmas brunch.

I can't remember exactly how it started. Instead of a big Christmas dinner, we have a big Christmas breakfast. Talk about your embarrassment of culinary riches. Our table is loaded with stuff we all like to eat.

Since we are all turkeyed out after Thanksgiving, we get one of those hickory baked hams from that place on South Santa Fe and Belleview. We have never been disappointed with those hams.

It's great for leftovers, too. We make pinto bean soup with the bone, scalloped potatoes with the ham bits, ham salad for sandwiches, and I love grilled ham slices with fried hominy.

Our brunch is rich in its diversity because we also pig out on bagels, cream cheese, red onions and lox. Trish is the best egg scrambler on the planet. They are light, fluffy and steamy. She fries up a mess of sausage, too.

Of course we have all sorts of Christmas pastries, including fruitcake, which I adore. I don't understand why fruitcake is disliked by so many folks. Some people say they are only good for doorstops. I love it, though. The Entenmann's fruitcakes are super. Not quite as good as Grandma Wilson baked, but super anyhow.

Trish found some special Christmas coffee we are having this morning, and we are popping corks on some bottles of cheap champagne, too. My son, Jon, looks forward to the Christmas brunch so much that he fasts the day before.

We do a lot of laughing on Christmas. The bubbly probably helps some. Of course we are all seeing Christmas through Jacob's eyes.

I'll never forget our first Christmas in Bear Valley. Brett and Jon were just little squirts then. Now they are in their mid-40s. Jon had decided he didn't believe in Santa Claus anymore and would stay up all night to see if old Nick would come to our house and somehow get the bicycles they wanted down the chimney. Jon was always a skeptical cuss. Still is.

There he sat by the fireplace in the big red chair. I thought he would never go to sleep. He and I played board games until 3 in the morning. I was exhausted. I could hardly stay awake myself. Finally, he fell asleep, and I scurried out to the garage where I had hidden two Stingray bicycles. Money was tight in those days, but Trish and I managed the bikes.

Somehow, I got them into the house and by Jon without waking him. Then, I tiptoed upstairs and got into bed just in time to hear Jon run upstairs and into his and Brett's room.

He said, "Brett! Brett! Wake up! Santa Claus was here and he brought us bicycles!"

When he thinks about it today, he says, "I just couldn't believe it. I couldn't believe Santa Claus had brought us those bikes." Let me tell you, that was some kind of merry Christmas, as is this one.

We all hope your Christmas is as happy as ours this morning.

December 26

Trish, my wife, needs to soldier on, live a fulfilling life

BALLOONED.

I feel sort of woozy this morning. "Woozy" is a made-up word our family used for years to describe it when we have the blahs. I guess "blahs" is also a made-up word, too, but you get the idea.

I'm alone today. Trish is having lunch with a friend at the Gemini restaurant on North Wadsworth. She still socializes with people with whom she worked at Exempla Hospice. I have encouraged her to do more of this.

She needs to get away from me, from this house and from this death-watch every now and then. This is true with all caregivers. I am urging her to plan what she will do after I die. I want her to travel with friends and to seek new social outlets.

Trish is much younger than I and ought to have a full life ahead of her and not remain in a perpetual state of mourning. She is very resourceful, and I think she'll be fine.

Getting back to today and my wooziness, I just called the Cody Dental Clinic to cancel my appointment with hygienist Patty Hull to get my teeth cleaned. My teeth are clean enough for what is left of my life.

Patty was trained by the late Dr. William Hiatt, a world-class periodontist. He saved my chops years ago when my gums ballooned painfully with an infection. My dentist then was an old pal, Dr. Len Kowalski. He referred me to Hiatt, who really cracked the whip when it came to care of gums.

Now, I am a real nut on dental care, brushing my teeth at least three times a day, using a toothpick after every meal and brushing with a special fluoride gel. All this hygiene hasn't made me live any longer, but I have great teeth.

Maybe it is genetic. When I was a little squirt, I remember Great Grandpa Billy Fiedler dying at the age of 91. After the funeral, some of his Grand Army of the Republic (Civil War) pals came to the house to pay their respects.

I was walking around and looking up at them as they talked. I can remember hearing them say, "He still had his own teeth." As a little kid, I didn't understand why they would say something like that after his funeral.

After breakfast this morning, I noticed I am about out of toothpaste. Should I try to make what is left last me to the end, or should I have Trish squander a few bucks for another tube? I know that seems needlessly frugal, but that's the way I am about my personal needs.

Trish thinks that's foolish. I'm not a tightwad about spending money on others. My family and friends will tell you I am generous to a fault. It's just that I can't stand wasting money on myself. It must have something to do with growing up during the Great Depression.

It's cold this morning, and I have turned on the gas fireplace that is supposed to look real. I feel guilty about that. I am here alone and there is no one else to share in my extravagance. To hell with that. I'll just enjoy it by myself.

While I am sitting here and coping with my wooziness, I am munching on some licorice Mary Chandler sent me. She is our art critic and one of our best writers. Some time back, we discovered our mutual love of licorice.

Little things like licorice mean a lot when you are in my situation. Thank you, Mary. Thank you.

I'm usually tired, but (surprise!) I'm still working out

HUNK.

Friends seem almost embarrassed to ask how I feel. How are you supposed to feel when you are dying? In a word: tired. Yes, that's it, I feel tired most of the time.

I still wake up at 3:30 every morning out of habit. I was in early morning radio for so long my internal clock is set that way. Now, though, pain wakes me up. After a milliliter of morphine, I go back into a deep sleep, waking up again about 7 a.m.

After shaving, showering and taking care of my other personal needs, I have breakfast, read the *Rocky*, watch the war on CNN for an hour and then I take my morning nap. Even with all that sleep, I still doze often, sometimes even when I am writing an entry in this diary.

Friends usually get around to asking about pain. I am taking four different pain medications that pretty well protect me from severe pain. Sure, I hurt all the time, but the medications make it possible for me to function.

This may surprise you, but I am still taking fitness training. Before I decided to quit taking medications that were only prolonging my agony, I bought a Bow-Flex weight machine.

You've seen it on TV. I never got to the point where I looked like that 40-year-old hunk who models with the Bow-Flex. I think it helped me, though. Angie, my trainer and massage therapist, helps me work with it.

It seems silly, I suppose, that a wrinkled, thin old man who is getting ready to die is working out on a Bow-Flex. I also do curls with eight-pound weights. I was up to 12 pounds before, but not anymore.

I figure I should be doing the best I can with what I have left. And I do think it makes me feel better. I am having a terrible time with my posture. Gravity is winning and I am losing. I keep trying not to slump, though.

In addition to being tired, I have dizzy spells. I have to be careful not to fall going up and down stairs. The other day I became dizzy for no apparent reason. I looked around and found my oxygen tube had become disconnected.

I have been on oxygen for many years because of my pulmonary fibrosis, which is an irreversible growth in my lungs. I don't think I'll ever get accustomed to having a 50-foot tube hooked up to my nose.

There is some curiosity about my pain medication. Do I get a "rush" from morphine? No. I can't imagine myself using any of these drugs for recreational purposes. They just give me relief from pain.

Back during World War II, we had packs of single morphine doses to be used to keep a wounded soldier from going into shock. I never heard of anyone using them for any other purpose, as was the case in the Vietnam War.

Morphine doesn't seem to be affecting my thinking process. I can feel its presence, though. It's a sort of deadening feeling around the back of my skull. It is in no way pleasant.

There are other side effects from drugs. Dry skin is a problem. I have had good luck with Vaseline Intensive Care lotion and Mennen's Baby Magic lotion. My lips become dry and chapped. I find Vaseline works better than ChapStick.

My hospice nurse gave me a little tip about my dry mouth problems. She said lemon candy drops help. They are the same lemon drops I remember from desert training in the Army that we took to prevent us from getting dry mouth and throat.

If it's OK with you, I think I'll end this diary page now and go upstairs for a little snooze.

January 1

Hey, what if I don't depart on time?

WHAT IF ...

I don't die? Of course we'll all die, but what if I don't die fairly soon? Embarrassing. That doesn't seem likely, but the thought has occurred to me as these last weeks drag on. It's possible my health might improve sufficiently for me to withdraw from hospice.

Then, what do I write in this diary? Maybe, "Sorry, folks, to have alarmed you, and sorry that Mayor Webb has named a street after me, but I'm OK now."

It's not likely. My weight is down to 127 from 170. I am exhausted most of the time, and I sleep and sleep and sleep some more. And when I wake up, I go back to sleep.

What little memory is left is about shot. My temper is getting shorter. I snap at Trish and am sorry the minute I do. None of my clothing fits anymore. Trish had to go to Dillard's to get me a new pair of pants for the street-naming ceremony because all my old britches fit me like a sock on a rooster.

I never understood that metaphor, but my father used it all the time. It seems to fit here, however, for some crazy reason I don't understand.

Mangled metaphors aside, some of my readers don't think I should give up and die.

Carol Hummel is one of them. She is a Christian Scientist and was kind enough to send me a copy of *Science and Health* by Mary Baker Eddy, which was copyrighted in 1890.

She was founder of Christian Science and of the Church of Christ, Scientist. She was severely injured in 1866. She was healed while reading about one of Jesus' healings in Matthew 9:1-8.

My grandmother, Nora Amole, was a Christian Scientist and walked to the First Christ Scientist Church just a few blocks from her home on West Maple Avenue. I don't believe the church is still there. If there is a heaven, Grandma is there and she is smiling because of Ms. Hummel's kindness.

The latter writes, "The reading/studying of this book has healed folks of all kinds of diseases, including cancer. You, too, can be healed!"

Frosty Wooldridge wants to make me live longer, too. He asks me to log onto www.oasiswellness.com. Despite my fragile condition, Frosty writes: "Damn, you still look like you could run a mile up hill and go skiing! I saw you on TV today."

Oasis Wellness, according to Frosty, "possesses cutting edge science that could radically help you gain a year or more of health and quality living. They have 10 patents on botanicals that raise your CHEA levels, which, in turn, improves your entire metabolic rate so you gain health, energy, vibrancy and much more.

"Their aloe vera improves your colon health dramatically and cleans your liver, which is generally very toxified in America from eating so much poison in our foods. Once your liver is clean, your health will improve. Their ginkgo biloba will get you off that Coumadin drain-cleaner crap. That stuff is doing you more harm than good."

I don't know, Frosty, I think I am too far gone for that strategy, but maybe it will help someone else. I guess when you get right down to the bottom line, I don't really want to live in pain any longer. Sure, there are things I would like to do, places I would like to see, other folks I would like to know, but the hour is late.

I am mentally and emotionally prepared to die. I keep finding myself referring to Scriptures, and today I turn to Ecclesiastes 2:16: "To every person there is a season, and to every purpose under the heaven. A time to be born and a time to die; a time to plant, and a time to pluck up that which is planted …"

Frosty, I think it is a time for me to die.

January 2

Old war buddies face one last challenge: saying goodbye

CHOKED UP.

It was so hard, so hard for both of us when I told Paul Allen I was dying. Trish and I were about to go out for dinner when the phone rang.

"Is that you, Frank?" the voice said. I knew right away it was Paul. I was always Frank in the Army because that's my first name. It doesn't make any difference what your mamma calls you, the Army calls you what is printed on your service record.

I had dreaded getting this phone call. Paul and I had talked every Christmas season since our old 6th Armored Division didn't need us anymore. We had been through so much together: desert training at Camp Coxcomb in the Mojave Desert and armored maneuvers at Camp Cooke, Calif.

Overseas, we were at Ramsden-Heath in England and Radnorshire in Wales, and then came the hard part: all five European Theater campaigns, Normandy, Northern France, Ardennes, Rhineland and Central Europe.

There were times when we thought it would never end. In writing about our old 6th Armored, General George Patton, our 3rd Army commander, referred to us as his "iron men." Let me tell you something, there were many times when we didn't feel like iron men. We were just kids, some of us still in our teens.

When you eat, sleep, fight and dig trenches together, you become close. When you are scared half out of your wits and look to one another for strength and courage, you know the true meaning of friendship.

Paul and I saw each other only once after the war. I stopped off to see him in New York in 1950 on my way back to Europe to write about what old battlefields were like five years after the shooting stopped. He and his wife, Eddie, entertained me at dinner at their Mount Vernon home.

Still, we talked every Christmas season about our work, our families and how our lives were changing. He had only one son, Bill, who was born while Paul and I were aboard the USS *Henrico* on our way to England.

After he retired, Paul and Eddie moved to Florida. They seemed to like it, despite all the hurricanes, fires and other distractions that are a part of life in Florida.

When we started to talk on the phone, he asked how I was feeling. I had to tell him I am dying. I got all choked up, and so did he. I tried to explain I was being cared for in a hospice program.

Paul had heard of hospice. He thought it was a place, though. I find a lot of people believe that. I explained it is care managed for a patient's comfort when he is dying. I told him I expected to die at home unless my care became too difficult for Trish, and then I would move to a hospice residence.

He asked about my pain. I told him drugs keep me reasonably comfortable.

We were able to laugh again at some of our old adventures, like that time on the outskirts of Brest, France, when we took out a flak tower the Germans were using as an observation post. We remembered how old Ralph Wharlow drove our half-track in reverse at 45 mph to keep us from getting killed.

Paul said his congressman gave him a medal for fighting at Normandy. He wanted to know if I got one, too. I didn't. Doesn't matter now. I don't need medals.

Then we said goodbye. Damn, that was so hard.

January 3

Living out my days in Marston Slopes

PROVISO.

Trish and I never expected to leave Denver. The only times I was ever away from Denver for any length of time were during World War II and the Korean War. I was born in Denver. So was my father. Our roots are deep in this town. All our kids were born here and attended Denver Public Schools.

Some guys with whom I worked in radio left Denver for network opportunities in larger cities. I never heard the call to go big time. I didn't even wonder if I could have made it had I tried.

Trading Denver for a job opportunity elsewhere never was a real possibility for me. As it turned out, my choice was a wise one. I have probably done better here than I would have elsewhere.

So why am I living out what's left of my life in Lakewood? One evening some years back we were driving along Wadsworth and Trish said, "I wonder what's up on that hill?" The hill is really a community called Marston Slopes.

Right on top was its oldest house with a lot of trees around it and a for-sale sign in the front yard. "How much do they want for it?" she wondered. Well, I called up the Realtor the next day and she showed us the house.

The view of the foothills from the kitchen window was gorgeous. I made an offer and it was accepted, and here we are. It wasn't easy to leave Bear Valley where Trish and I lived and raised our kids.

I had to find room for my instant family after I remarried. I had a terrible time locating a house to rent, and I couldn't afford to buy one. Lloyd Knight, my old radio sidekick for years, told me about a house that was for sale in his block on South Depew Street.

He said it had been on the market for six months and maybe the guy would rent it to me. The guy did, but with the proviso that after six months, I either had to buy the house or move.

I was backed into the corner and had to take the deal. We moved in the kids and what sparse furniture Trish and I had in our apartment. After the six months were up, I borrowed money to float the second mortgage, and there we stayed for 30 years.

Sure, we had many wonderful friends and neighbors and hated to leave them, but we weren't moving all that far away, and we still see them in the old Bear Valley Shopping Center, what's left of it, anyhow.

We figured with the twilight years just ahead, why not do something for ourselves? That's about the best explanation I can give. Of course I wasn't thinking about dying here, but everyone has to die somewhere.

It's a nice diverse neighborhood with Asian, Anglo, African American and Hispanic families. When we moved here, there weren't many children, mostly retired families. Lately, though, younger families are moving in, and I just love hearing children laughing and playing again.

I do have to tell you about the nicest thing that happened to me the other day. The Marston Slopes Homeowners Association voted to name our little park, "Gene Amole Park" because I lived here and loved the park.

I should be thanking them for making this such a fine place to live with such caring neighbors.

January 9
Meeting jazz hero strikes happy chord

SPUNK.

You know what's really great? It's when you finally meet someone you have respected and admired for many years, and he is everything you imagined him to be. That was my reaction when I finally met Johnny Smith, one of my generation's best jazz guitarists.

I have mentioned him several times in my diary, and how my memories of old 17th Street involve Shaner's Bar and Grill just off Welton Street where he used to perform. In my mind I can still hear him playing that lovely ballad, "Moonlight in Vermont."

Sure, I had seen him play many times, but I never had enough spunk to introduce myself to tell him how I enjoyed his music so much. I played his recordings on my jazz radio show, "Amole after Dark."

I also mentioned how our mutual friend, Max DiJulio, composed some ballet music for a television documentary on the arts I wrote and how Johnny and flutist Pam Endsley recorded it for me. Still, I had never met him.

It took several friends to finally get us together. Johnny is retired now and living in Colorado Springs. He had heard about my column through a friend at a weekly newspaper and decided to contact me.

First, his friend called my son, Brett, and then my daughter, Tustin, aka Muffy. I finally got Johnny's phone number and called him. Meanwhile, Suzanne Weiss, a former *Rocky* City Hall reporter, began combing the Internet for his recording of "Moonlight in Vermont."

She found one, also featuring Stan Getz, and mailed it to me. What a friend she has been through the years! She is the Catholic girl who sat next to me in the newsroom. I always tried to sit next to a Catholic girl at work because they know how to spell and I don't.

Johnny and I finally got together. He was kind enough to tackle I-25 for coffee and sweet rolls in my kitchen. What a great time we had!

He doesn't miss traveling, playing at big jazz parties and all-star concerts. "I always liked the more intimate places like Shaner's," he told me.

Funny thing, though, if it wasn't for the old U.S. Army, he might not have become the famous jazz artist he is.

Johnny had a pilot's license before he went into the Army and assumed he would be accepted for training in what was then the Army Air Forces and then would later become an airline pilot. No go, though. He had a minor problem with one of his eyes and was given the choice of joining the Army band or going to mechanics school.

He opted for the band even though he knew military marching bands don't have guitar players. His sergeant gave him a trumpet and told him to go into the latrine and learn to play it by himself in two weeks, or it was off to mechanics school.

What a wonderful career he has had. He doesn't miss it, though. He loves to fish and spend time with his family, and he is proud of the fact he has two great grandchildren.

Here I am on my last legs, and I finally got to meet one of my heroes. He said we'll talk again.

January 10

A surefire way to avoid the chill of the grave

ASHES.

Here is one old grandpa who doesn't want to be dry-iced into perpetuity.

I love Ann Carnahan's "Whatever Happened To …" series in the *Rocky*, particularly her recent story about Bredo Morstoel, who is frozen rock-solid in Nederland.

His grandson, Trygve Bauge, had the old man frozen in 1989 with the hope medical science will one day revive him. His body is kept at 75 degrees below zero with 1,500 pounds of dry ice every month.

Trygve must be in the big bucks. He has spent 130 grand to keep the corpse iced down. This process is called cryogenics, and I want no part of it. When my legs finally give out, I have authorized my friend, John Horan, to cremate what is left and inter it at Fort Logan where most of my old buddies are now resting.

Have I mentioned how difficult it is for old people to stay warm? I can feel a draft if the window in the house next door is open. It's my kind of luck that Trish is a fresh-air devotee, but we have worked it out so there are warm zones in our dwelling.

My dislike of cold weather goes back to Bastogne, Belgium, where I spent the 1944 winter during the Big War. I haven't been warm since. Frost didn't just bite me, it damn near chewed off my hands and feet.

Trish bought me some Wyoming Wear fleece socks that help some. I have a goose-down parka and mukluks, none of which fits me anymore because I have lost so much weight.

When I read Annie's story, I was reminded of the poetry of vagabond Robert W. Service, who chronicled in verse the trials and tribulations of hearty prospectors who pioneered the Yukon. How I loved those poems when I was a kid!

Service is best known for his "The Shooting of Dan McGrew." His poetry inspired Herndon Davis to paint the face on the barroom floor at Central City. My book of his poetry has 735 pages. They were more than just poems, they were sagas.

So many of them had cold weather as a theme. My two favorites are "The Cremation of Sam McGee" and "The Ballad of Blasphemous Bill McKie." McGee tells his pal, "Yet 'tain't being dead—it's my awful dread of the icy grave that pains; so I want you to swear that, foul or fair, you'll cremate my last remains."

And that's what his pal does in a huge fire built from their cabin. He stuffs in old Sam "looking cool and calm in the heart of the furnace roar; And wore a smile you could see a mile, and he said, 'Please close that door. It's fine in here, but I greatly fear that you'll let in the cold and storm—Since I left Plumtree, down in Tennessee, it's the first time I've been warm.'"

McKie had a different problem. His pal promised to bury him "Whenever, wherever or whatsoever the manner of death he die." When he found old Bill, he was frozen solid, "Hard as a log and trussed like a frog, with his arms and legs outspread."

His pal asks, "Have you ever stood in an Arctic hut in the shadow of the Pole with a little coffin six by three and a grief you can't control? Have you ever sat with a frozen corpse that looks at you with a grin and seems to say, 'You may try all day, but you'll never jam me in'?"

What to do? "So I sawed off poor Bill's arms and legs, and I laid him snug and straight in a little coffin he picked hisself with the dinky silver plate, and I came nigh near shedding a tear as I nailed him safely down. Then I stowed him away on my Yukon sleigh, and I started back to town ..."

No cryogenics for this old grandpa. Cremation and Fort Logan will be fine for me.

January 12

Of actuarial tables and soldiering on

LIMBO.

I woke up this morning from a two-hour nap and didn't die, damn it! It was stated more eloquently in I Corinthians 15:55: "O death, where is thy sting? O grave, where is thy victory?"

Can we talk? Sure, it would be nice to die quietly while taking a nap, but it isn't likely that will happen. That's what my hospice nurse tells me. Predicting when I shall die is risky business.

I don't have a terminal disease like cancer or a heart that isn't functioning. She tells me I have a "failure to thrive." The systems that have been keeping me alive all these years are gradually shutting down.

The symptoms are obvious. I continue to lose weight. I have difficulty staying awake. My strength is ebbing away. I am in constant pain. My blood supply is out of whack.

Still, I'm hanging on even though I don't want to be. This confounds the insurance company that would prefer I die on some kind of actuarial schedule it has worked up on a spreadsheet.

But no, I am in limbo, and there is nothing much I can do about it. My nurse tells me I can't will myself to die, but I shall know when death is near. I guess I am supposed to stand on tippy-toes and wait.

Grandpa Amole knew when he would die. He was living with us the last year of his life. He was a stoic old guy and never complained about anything. At his last supper, I recall how he rolled up his napkin and placed it in his napkin ring as deliberately as he had done thousands of times before.

Then Grandpa got up from the table and said, "I'm going upstairs and die." That's exactly what he did. He just climbed the stairs, walked into his room and got up on his bed and died. He didn't explain how he knew it was time to die. He just died. How I wish it were that simple.

I have conflicting emotions about what is happening to me. For some reason writing this diary has energized me. I wonder if it is keeping me alive when I should be dead. Should I just couch-potato it until I dry up and blow away?

Frankly, I am at a loss to explain the popularity of what I am doing. What's the big deal about Gene Amole dying? Everyone is going to die. You. Me. All of us.

As sick as I am, I am writing more than twice as much as I did before. Why is that? Is there really that much to say about getting ready to die? Is it easier than writing thumbsuckers about the war against terrorism?

Whatever the reason, I spend an inordinate amount of time sitting before this computer plumbing the depths of my feelings about death. Why? I don't know. I just want to get it over with, the sooner, the better.

I'll be seeing Dr. Jeanne Day Seibert for an evaluation. I value her opinion. I also want to talk to Dr. Ray Garrett, who has become a friend of mine through all of this.

I surely want to live long enough for him to take me to see and hear Ellyn Rucker sing and play at the Burnsley. He says he can get me close enough to the door so I can get in with my oxygen tank and all. That would make living in limbo a little easier to take.

January 15

Pain becomes ugly companion

THIRD BASE.

I hope I can somehow make it through this column. At the beginning of this project, I promised myself I wouldn't be goody two-shoes about death-and-dying all the time.

You know what I mean. It's the temptation of cranking out stuff that would make readers say to themselves, "Oh isn't he brave, facing death with humor and love and courage." That kind of garbage.

Let me tell you one thing: This has been one ugly day. You'll never know how ugly. The hospice people are constantly asking patients to rate their pain on a one-to-ten scale. They haven't asked me today, but if they did, I would have to say my agony is breaking through the 15 level.

It started early this morning when I had to ask Trish for help to get out of bed. I hate to have to ask for help like that, but God, I hurt all over. There wasn't one square inch of my body that didn't hurt.

I couldn't imagine what happened to me. Sure, I have pain all the time, but I have been able to bring it under control with morphine, Roxicet, or any other of the feel-better drugs I have at my disposal.

Not this time, though. Nothing worked. I had so wanted to have fun with Jacob, who spent the night with us. He'll be 6 next week and is just full of himself. He had brought over board games he wanted to play with me, but I was in so much pain I couldn't even concentrate on Monopoly.

I passed out this morning, and he was there when I awakened. I was in so much pain I couldn't walk alone. I needed someone to steady me. Trish asked Jacob if he would like to help me go to the bathroom.

"No thank you," he said, with that little straightforward smile on his face, obviously thinking more than just "helping me walk" was involved.

God, how I love that little kid. I was sorry I wasn't able to make flap-jacks for him, which he wants me to do when he spends the night on weekends.

Last night, though, he cleaned his plate of the boeuf bourguignon I whipped up for him yesterday. He still claims his daddy's beef bur-gundy is the best. But grandpa's is good, too, he says diplomatically.

I hadn't fixed it in a long time. The recipe is in *Morning*, my first book. Pierre Wolfe has included it in his new book. I remember fixing it for Pierre years ago when he was doing a cooking shtick on Channel 7.

I remember making the noodles from scratch for him. He probably didn't notice, figuring maybe I got them out of a cellophane bag. I guess I was showboating a little.

I hope Jim Trotter, my editor, and the copy desk folks are examining this column with a fine-tooth comb. My fingers are skittering out of control over the computer keyboard.

I guess I have made it almost to the bottom line without a serious meltdown, and I should probably quit while I am still ahead. I am rounding third and heading for home. Thank you for your patience and understanding, but this has been one hell of a day, and I probably would never have made it without Trish juicing me with a dab of morphine.

That's it, dear readers, I'm off to beddy-bye.

January 16

Skeleton in closet? Nope— you'll find him on the Bowflex

NUTTY.

Angie just left. You remember Angie Augdemberge. She is my massage therapist and personal trainer. It may seem crazy to you for a dying man to have a personal trainer, but it makes some kind of strange sense to me.

I am continuing to waste away. I stopped weighing myself when I dropped to 127. If I lose more weight, I don't want to know about it. I have decided to make the best use of what is left of me.

Angie says I am doing OK on the Bowflex machine I bought before I went into hospice. You must have seen the Bowflex advertisements on

TV. They show a handsome, muscular man as he lifts, pulls, pushes and otherwise punishes himself.

The devil is finding my mind a wonderful playground. I had a nutty idea while Angie was putting me through my paces today. I would get my son Brett, the photographer, to videotape me going through the same Bowflex routine while stripped to my skivvies and send it to the company.

You probably can't appreciate the humor in this unless you had seen me in the altogether. I look like a living skeleton. I thought about billing myself as Mr. Skin-and-Bones of 2002.

Of course I don't let anyone see me that way. When folks stop by, I bulk up by wearing heavy sweat shirts or sweaters. Whatever works, I say.

On another matter, I was thrilled to receive this snail-mail note:

"Dear friend Gene,

"It was so good to visit with you yesterday. It was such a bonus to get to meet your lovely wife and Tustin. No way to fully express my gratitude for the warm hospitality.

"I wish all of you a five-star 2002.

"I remain your friend for life,

"Johnny Smith."

I don't know if it is possible to die happy, but that letter from not only a great guitar player but a wonderful human being certainly will help.

It did something else. It offset an e-mail message I received from another Smith, someone named Ken Smith (obviously no relation). It said:

"As you told me—'Life isn't fair.' No one cares about your prattlings about the end of your miserable existence any more than they care about the injustices I have suffered.

"Suffer, you old f--t! You've earned it."

On the other hand, I was delighted to hear from Cindy Rogers Fair at Etobicoke, Ontario. Fifteen years ago, she was an exchange student living in our Bear Valley home while she attended the Career Education Center.

I wish you could have known her. What a wonderful girl (now a woman) she is. After teaching in Australia for a year, Cindy is back in Canada and the mother of a 3-month-old son. She'll send pictures. I can't wait.

And Trish stopped by Blockbuster. We'll watch *Planet of the Apes* and *Moulin Rouge*. Again, whatever works.

Amole family has left Tobacco Road

C OURAGE.

Now that I am on my way out, I am pleased the Amole family has reached a significant milestone: None of us smokes anymore.

My younger daughter, Susan, gave me the best gift I could have received: She finally kicked the habit. There is irony in this story, and I am sure she won't mind my telling it.

I smoked big time for more than 30 years. I was often a two-pack-a-day man. I also smoked a pipe and cigars. In the Army, I enjoyed an occasional chaw of Day's Work or Brown's Mule when it was dangerous to light up at night.

Smoking gave me a lot of pleasure. I liked the way it felt when I sucked smoke down into my lungs. For me, cigarettes were a necessity after a meal, with coffee and in conjunction with other activities, if you catch my meaning.

I enjoyed watching smoke snort from my nostrils. For me, a cigarette was a wonderful companion when I was lonely. I thought it was romantic to light a cigarette with mine for a lady friend.

So why did I quit? Did cancer scare me? No. The reason I quit was because I was 46 years old when Susan was born. From a practical sense, I figured I'd have to last longer to support her and pay for her college education. That was why I quit. It wasn't easy, but I did it cold turkey. I still dream of smoking.

So do you see the irony here? Brett never really smoked all that much. Jon must have quit about 10 years ago. Muffy quit 25 years ago. And so in recent years, Susan, for whom I quit, was the only one of us still hooked.

She probably was sick of my nagging her for years about it. I think she finally found the courage—and it takes courage—to quit, and I am proud of her as is her husband, Gary, and her adorable son, Jacob, in whom the sun rises and sets for all of us.

I haven't smoked a cigarette in 32 years, but I would like to have one right now, right this minute. When I quit, I carried a pack of cigarettes with me all the time in case I just had to have one. I kept cigarettes on the table by my bed, in my desk at the office, in the glove compartment of my car for the same reason.

There weren't patches or pills to help me quit then. My strategy was simple. I pitted my stubbornness against the utter stupidity of putting paper stuffed with dead leaves in my mouth and setting fire to it.

I never told myself I was quitting cigarettes forever. That was too daunting. I figured I was strong enough not to smoke that one cigarette I wanted at that moment. And that's the way I quit, one cigarette at a time, the way I have lived my life, one day at a time.

I was so pleased that Pat Larkin wrote from her home in Red Lodge, Montana, that she finally quit. Wow, I wonder how many Pall Malls I fired up for her when we were young.

But now that I am dying and Susan graduated from college years ago, and I liked smoking so much, why don't I light up a Marlboro? Why not just one more?

That's not an example I would want to set for Jacob. No sir. No way.

January 18

Bright lights, good memories

Transcribed.

I just turned on the Christmas tree lights. Yes, we still have a Christmas tree in the corner of our dining room. Maybe it is because this was my last Christmas that I don't want to let it go.

Some folks are so fond of their Christmas trees that they leave them up all year. Ellie Weckbaugh comes to mind. She was a wealthy socialite whose name often appeared in newspaper society columns years ago.

She was a lovely person, a patron of the arts and an all-around good gal. She was also deeply religious. I never saw it myself, but she supposedly was so fond of her Christmas tree that she left it decorated all year long.

She invited south Denver neighborhood kids to swim in her pool behind her home. It seems to me that Father Jim "Pope Jim" Sunderland was one of those kids.

I thought of her just this morning while going through my torrent of e-mail. In it was a friendly note from the Weckbaugh family who must have remembered a column I wrote about Ellie years ago.

This is the last night I'll get to see the tree. My son-in-law, Gary Waters, is coming over tomorrow to take it down. I loved the tree this year. Trish decided just to put white lights on it, no ornaments.

I didn't think I would like the idea. We have so many ornaments that have become traditional in our family. Once Gary had decorated the tree, though, I thought it was beautiful. As soon as it is dark enough in the late afternoon, I bend down and turn it on. The way the lights sparkle in the mirrors creates a sort of magic.

There used to be a tradition in Denver to leave Christmas decorations up until after Billy Saul's stock show. No more, though. Stock show visitors aren't likely to show up in our dining room, anyhow. Billy is the head publicist for the stock show. Did I mention his lovely wife, Judy, sent me Gummi Bears?

I guess there is nothing so over as Christmas when the last of the Entenmann's fruitcake is gone. There is just a sliver of it left from the fourth Entenmann's we had this year. It is carefully Saran-wrapped in the refrigerator and waiting for me as my midnight snack.

Speaking of midnight snacks, I hated it when I got down to the last anise pizzelle Italian cookies Rose Maroney baked for me. Why is it we have to wait for Christmas for pizzelle cookies? Is there some kind of spiritual significance I don't know about?

Before Rose came into my life, Vaud Welch baked them for me in her kitchen up on Floyd Hill. Vaud listened to my "Music for a New Day" program on the old KVOD.

By the way, readers have been asking for the name of my theme song then. It was the Trumpet Concerto in E Flat by Tomaso Albinoni. It followed the "Second Romanian Rhapsody" by George Enescu that closed the all-night program preceding mine.

If my memory serves me correctly, Albinoni wrote the E Flat Concerto for oboe and string orchestra. The amazing Maurice Andre had it transcribed for trumpet, which he played so elegantly.

A Highlander Boy says his prayers

RESPECT.

Gee, what a wonderful day this is for me. The sun is shining. The air is crisp. There are deep shadows in the foothills outside my window. It's a good day to write about prayer.

I'm alone in my study and listening to Bill Evans playing "What Is There To Say?" from a CD that Dr. Ray Garrett brought to me. Muffy gave me a little Timex AM/FM/CD player that also has forest, wind, surf and other nature sounds. It's just the right size for my little study, where I write. Nifty.

Now I'm able to listen to "Concerto for Geno," a CD of jazz pieces Bill Gallo and I both enjoy. He and his son produced it for me. Jerry Kopel also sent me a CD of "Music for Nighttime Dining or a Lazy Afternoon," a lovely medley of 37 standards. Someone else sent me a CD of Les Brown and His Band of Renown recorded at the Trocadero at Elitch Gardens years ago.

It's in here that I try to catch up on my e-mail. One reader wanted to know about the Highlander Boys, an organization that had a profound effect on my life and about the late George Olinger, its founder.

I joined the Highlanders when I was 8 and retired when I was 16. Olinger had great success as a mortician. Because it came as a result of death, he wanted to return something to the community that celebrated life.

He saw the need for a boys organization in the Highland section of North Denver. That's where the name Highlander Boys originated.

At first it was built around sports, but as the years passed it evolved into a fourfold program of mental, physical, social and spiritual development. Olinger believed that a quasi-military program could best meet those goals.

We dressed in uniforms resembling those worn by World War I American soldiers and were organized into squads, platoons, companies and battalions. We entered as recruits, rising to provisionals and then to uniformed Highlanders.

We learned the meaning of discipline within our ranks from our own noncommissioned and commissioned officers. A reserve U.S. Army officer served as commandant, and he was assisted by civilians responsible for character development.

We drilled once a week at the Temple of Youth at 300 Logan St. After the Highlanders lost the building during the Depression, it became the armory for the Colorado National Guard. It was razed and is now the site of Channel 9's studios.

The Reverend David Delaplane reminded me of Highlander spiritual development when he e-mailed me this copy of the Highlander Prayer, which we all committed to memory and said each night at bedtime:

"Oh, God, my father and my friend, teach me to be a true Highlander and a Christian gentleman.

Help me to think pure thoughts that I may be a clean man.

Help me to keep my body pure that I may use it to serve Thee.

Help me to be truthful that I may sing thy praise.

Help me to be honest that I may win the confidence of men.

Help me to build a Christian character that I may be worthy of those who love me.

Teach me to respect all women as I do my mother.

Make my life one of service, and when I am tempted,

May I sit humbly at the foot of the cross and look up to Thee for strength. Amen."

January 23

Snuggling up to my Peggy Lee memories

FEVER.

I am writing this at 4:30 Tuesday morning and remembering how soft and cuddly Peggy Lee was. That's the way I shall always think of her, soft and cuddly. She had fallen into my arms, and in the briefest of time I held her, I still remember how soft and cuddly she was.

I couldn't sleep this morning and was listening to National Public Radio and was surprised to hear her singing Fever. The BBC announcer was reporting her death. She was 81 and had died in California. The story was right up there with stories of an attack at a U.S. cultural center in India.

Everyone knew Peggy Lee, but not everyone had held her in their arms as I did that frosty morning at 16th Street and Glenarm Place in Denver. It was by accident that I found out how soft and cuddly she was.

She was standing on a cardboard box and was trying to make an announcement over a public address microphone. It had been rigged up so folks could see celebrities during the Red Feather campaign.

Most folks have forgotten that the Community Chest or United Way campaign started here in Denver. It was Bob Selig's idea to make the red feather the symbol of United Way, but I can't remember now why he chose the red feather.

He was a fireball kind of guy and no one ever questioned him. He designated me the Red Feather man, and I made announcements on 16th Street every hour of how the campaign was going. He made me dress up in a red feather costume. That's how I happened to be with Peggy Lee. It was silly, but I went along with it because Bob was a neat guy, a real slam-bang go-getter.

Peggy Lee was just getting started. I loved her recording of "Why Don't You Do Right" with Benny Goodman. She was wearing a green velvet coat and hat that day. Sweet. Very sweet. She smiled at me when I caught her, falling from the cardboard box, and to this day, I think I detected a little snuggle.

I suspect the Bravo channel will rerun that show she recorded maybe 15 years or so ago. I hope so. Her performance was timeless. Sure, her face was very tight from all the cosmetic surgery, but that's OK, right?

Little Norma Egstrom from North Dakota had style, real style, didn't she? And her voice held up didn't it? Sure it did. You betcha! She had fever, real fever.

Somewhere in my stack of CDs, I have that one where she sings the blues. I'll get it out and play it tonight with that one where she sings with the BG sextet. That will be my private tribute to her.

I'm sure I have some other Peggy discs I'll hear, including "Is That All There Is?" At this point in my life, I have been asking myself the same question.

I don't know what ever happened to Bob Selig after he moved to Southern California to run the movie industry, but I shall always be indebted to him. Not for making me wear that funny red feather suit, but for making it possible for me to hold that soft and cuddly Peggy Lee.

Thanks, Bob, wherever you are.

That's all there is.

January 24

So much joy found in one little boy

HERKY-JERKY.

There were 10 little kids laughing and hollering in Susan's patio room as one of them was swinging a baseball bat at a Mickey Mouse pinata hanging from the roof. Smack! went the bat against Mickey's face, and little bags of candy and small toys splattered out across the floor.

The kids giggled and laughed as they reached for the goodies to put in little paper bags. After the pinata was smashed to pieces, and the kids had scooped up most of the souvenirs, Jacob came over to me and took my hand. He helped me from my chair and took me to a clown's hat and gave it to me.

It was his sixth birthday party, and he wanted me to have something to remember it by. No one told him to do it. He just did it on his own. Let me tell you something, his kindness got me all choked up. I walked away and sat down and wiped the tears from my eyes so no one would see me crying.

How I love that little kid! After I had the clown's hat, he went back to play with the other kids. They were playing pin-the-red-nose-on-the-clown. He was laughing because all the blindfolded kids somehow pinned the nose on the clown's face, and all of them received prizes.

After the games, the kids scarfed up pizza and a chocolate cake shaped like a car. Then they went into the living room where they opened Jacob's presents. Trish and a couple of the kids' mothers helped scoop up wrappers as Susan tried to keep track of who sent the presents for thank you notes.

Finally, the parents came by to pick up their kids. Sunday was a wonderful day for Jacob and for me, and I was exhausted. When it was time for Trish and me to go home, Jacob put his arms around me and told me he loved me.

That was my weekend.

My hospice nurse came today and we discussed the possible causes for my depression and what could be done to lessen it, if anything.

Tremors in my hands and arms continue to slow me down. I have to go back and write every word over and over again sometimes. The Inderol I am taking helps some.

I don't know where I would be without the spell check on my computer when my hands go herky-jerky.

Steve Blatt called this evening and said he and Charley Samson will come to see me Friday afternoon. I am looking forward to that. I have been saving a letter I received from Al Sipes who used to be the night man on KVOD.

Whoops! There goes my herky-jerky hands again. Charley wondered what happened to Al.

We used to call him Weird Al. Turns out he is OK and is praying for me. He would call me in the old days to wake me up in the morning so I could get coffee and doughnuts and do "Music for a New Day." He and his wife, Cathy, live in Loveland now. They have been married 37 years.

The only programs from the old KVOD that have survived were Charley Samson's Mozart programs that are now heard during the midday Mozart program on the new KVOD on public radio. Thank goodness for that. There is no one in this town who knows more about W.A. Mozart than Charley.

You can take that to the bank. Now, I am off to bed.

January 26

Writing helps me cope with waiting

COCOONED.

"I love the snow glistening on the foothills," I said to my editor, Jim Trotter, on the telephone.

"There's the first line of your column," he said to me. I had called to see how many columns were left in my pipeline.

"No one said you had to crank out a column every day," Jim said. "Three a week would be just fine. That's what the other guys are doing.

Or you could do less." I told him I was writing one a day because there seemed to be so much to say about death and dying.

What I didn't tell him was that writing so much helped me cope with the prospect of dying. It was giving me something to do in my world of sitting around and waiting to die.

I know this seems crazy, but here I am cocooned with nothing to do but be a couch potato. I am sick of watching the war on CNN and eating cottage cheese when I am hungry.

Thank heavens for my family. Brett came over yesterday to ask my advice on fixing the bathroom in my old north Denver house. This morning, before I opened my eyes to see the snowy panorama outside my kitchen window, Jon was cleaning my sidewalks and driveway. What great sons I have.

I once complained about that chore, but I secretly cherished it. I miss the snowflakes sticking to my spectacles and the tingling pain on my frostbitten fingertips.

I spent about 10 minutes on the telephone with Susan. Sometimes I let my personal life slip over into my public life, and I shouldn't do that. I ought to be able to keep them separate, you know what I mean?

It is difficult to write personal commentary without hurting the feelings of members of my family. I have never wanted to hurt anyone's feelings, even folks I don't particularly care for. Wow! My mom would squirm at ending that awkward sentence with a preposition.

I started to write this column about Harry Smith, with whom I chatted recently on the telephone. Dusty Saunders did a nice column about him in a recent "Spotlight."

I understand Harry's despair about wanting to report on America's war on terrorism. I felt the same way in 1950 during the Korean War. I jumped right in then and did radio broadcasts and *Denver Post* articles from the battlefields.

Looking back at it, I don't think my work made one whit of difference. I was just a little guy pretending to be a big-time war correspondent. While I thought my stuff was right on the mark, I don't believe anyone else gave a damn.

It didn't matter, though, because no one paid much attention to the war anyhow. Maybe folks don't really care about the war on terrorism, either, so long as it doesn't poop in their Post Toasties.

From my standpoint, it's OK if Harry continues to bring his considerable talent to work on documentaries for the History and A&E channels. I find myself watching them more than the network sitcoms with laugh-track responses to not-so-funny jokes.

Harry is for real. That's what makes him special, believable.

January 30

Sleep just kind of sneaks up on me

NEURONTIN.

Geez, I'm a little woozy and don't know if I'm up to writing a page for my diary or not. It's been windy all morning and hearing it whistle through the pines outside my window makes me so sleepy.

I slept all day yesterday and didn't wake up until 2 this morning on the couch in the family room. The gas fireplace was on and so I was warm. I don't know what time Trish went to bed, but she left the TV on. She had left the sound on low, and it didn't wake me up. When I turned it off, a lady was pitching some kind of infomercial.

When I woke up again, I had breakfast about 8:30. Talk about a lost day. I looked at the log where I keep track of the drugs I take, and I hadn't taken any morphine or Roxicet the whole day. It must be the added strength of Neurontin that's knocking me out of my socks.

I am now taking three 600mg tablets a day. The side effects must be getting more sleep and dry mouth. I keep a cup of ice water next to me all the time to sip when my mouth gets so dry I can't even speak. The licorice Suzanne Weiss brought to me helps, too.

It has been quiet here all day. If the phone has rung, Trish must have answered it because I have been out of the world. As I write this, it is about 10 in the morning. I was hungry when I awakened, and so I had a dish of cottage cheese to help me get along until lunch. I find I have cultivated a taste for cottage cheese. Have I mentioned this before?

Trish has been up in her little study trying to organize certain details of her life after I die. By that I mean how she will take care of her finances and insurance obligations. She is good at this kind of thing.

She has three-ring binder notebooks all ready with index tabs so she can thumb for information when she needs it.

It's a great comfort to me that she is this well-organized. When I realized I was going to die, I worried about how she would get along without me. I guess most dying husbands feel this way.

I just didn't want to roll over and die and leave her with a passel of problems, you know what I mean? I have seen this happen before, and it's not a pretty picture for the widow to have to meet these obligations without any preparations.

In my case, I have always handled all the bills without any participation with her. That was so wrong. I should have involved her in all this years ago, but I didn't and now I am trying to play catch-up.

It would have been so much easier if she had been involved with our finances from the beginning. I know some guys who have let their wives handle all the family's finances. I suppose there is danger in that, too.

I guess each family should develop a strategy best for it. The trick is to not let death catch up on you with no preparation for the years that follow for those left behind.

I just popped another Neurontin tablet, and I better hurry up with this before I get woozy again. Sleep just sort of sneaks up on me, and before I know it, I'm up on my bed and out of action, so to speak.

My hospice nurse is coming at 2:30 this afternoon, and I should try to be up and at 'em for her. That's it for now.

As the little cartoon rabbit says, "So long, folks!"

January 31

Parents' vicarious ways foul vision of the game

CORRUPTED.

There is nothing new in brawling parents at kids' hockey games. The incident at the South Suburban Family Sports Center reminded me of problems I faced more than 20 years ago when I was head man at the Southwest Denver Little League Baseball.

I was dragged into it kicking and screaming by well-meaning fathers who were trying to organize Little League Baseball for their kids. "Look,

Mr. Amole," one of the fathers said, "we need someone with a name folks know and recognize. You won't have to do anything. We'll take care of everything."

Ha! What a bunch of malarkey that was. By the end of the summer, I was out at least $2,500, and half the parents in Bear Valley wouldn't speak to me. I had to admit my own 2 sons put pressure on me to be the commissioner.

Being commissioner meant I had to take 500 kids and put them into teams that were organized by draft. That's when the trouble began. The fathers were scrapping over kids they knew were talented players, leaving the others out.

I had no idea this was happening. When the drafting began, I started to realize what was going on here was a battle between fathers to see who had the best kids. As the season went on, it became clear I was watching games between fathers, not kids. They were just pawns on a grown-up chess board.

I realized in many cases the fathers were using their kids to live out their own unresolved ambitions to be winners on the baseball diamond. I saw this over and over again. Of the 500 kids in our program, I saw only 2 who made it to the big leagues, and they made it only for a cup of coffee.

Somehow, we had organized the games so that we had taken the fun out of their play. If I had to do it all over again, I would have stayed on the sidelines and let them organize their own teams and their own play.

Maybe they would have had more fun without the fancy uniforms we supplied them. I think we were forcing them into being adults too fast. We should have just let them be kids. We shouldn't have robbed them of their childhood.

I was so ashamed of ourselves when we had to protect our umpires and escort them to their cars when rowdy parents didn't like their calls. I can remember one incident when one of our star pitchers came to me to turn in his uniform.

I asked him why he was quitting the game. He said his manager (one of the fathers who coached the team) told him to throw at the head of the star batter on the other team. "I just couldn't do it," he said to me.

I thought to myself, "What are we doing here? How have we let a game played by little boys corrupt their lives?" I was proud of him for the decision he made. All these years later, he is an executive in a large Colorado corporation, and the jerk who wanted him to throw at another player went nowhere in life.

I truly love the game of baseball. I hate how it has evolved into a sport that is controlled by who has the most money. I suspect we have let this happen even down at the Little League level. We have forgotten that it is the game that is important. It is the game we love, not the monsters who have corrupted it.

February 1
Hawaii, Paris are beckoning

LAPTOP.

May I touch base on a few items important to me this morning?

Good. Fortified by 10mg of Inderal, I was awarded an Honorary Graduation Diploma from the Charles McLain Community High School of Jefferson County, Class of 2002, yesterday morning.

You may recall I lacked sufficient credit hours to be graduated from South High School in Denver back in 1941. I was graduated anyhow based upon a promise I would make up those hours in summer school that year. I didn't. World War II had something to do with it. So did my first job in radio.

Nevertheless, I have felt guilty ever since my promise to South speech teacher Leon K. Whitney went unfulfilled. I loved the old guy, and I am still ashamed I let him down. My speech that night in my blue suede suit went OK, though.

My friend Mark Stevens, public relations officer for Denver Public Schools, e-mailed me that South High is ready to forgive me and also wishes to grant me a diploma. Details are pending.

The diploma I received from McLain yesterday takes into account my life experiences in journalism and in the real world. I was deeply moved by the ceremony in my home because McLain also honored my old pal, Harry Farrar, with similar recognition before he died.

Harry was a legitimate wordsmith at *The Denver Post* for many years. He was a high school dropout and finally reached his goal as a graduate when McLain granted him a diploma. His tired old eyes filled with tears when he told me of his diploma.

McLain is a Jefferson County option school and one of Colorado's finest providers of nontraditional/alternative education. It has been providing Jeffco students with viable pathways to earning a high school diploma for more than 30 years.

Item No. 2: My old pal Jim Conrad tells me his bronze sculpture is now on display at the firehouse of Engine No. 1, Ladder 24, overlooking Ground Zero in New York. It is a rendering of that famous Record of Bergen, N.J., photograph of firefighters looking up at an American flag.

Father Chris Keenan, who succeeded Father Mychal Judge, killed in the Sept. 11 attack, told Jimbo in a brogue thick enough to be cut with a very sharp knife that the sculpture is so honored by the firefighters that it has been moved to the second floor of the firehouse where it will be safe.

It is properly displayed there so it isn't a temptation for thieves who want to profit from the 9-11 tragedy.

Item No. 3: Have you noticed how wretchedly cold it is? It is too damned cold for this dying old man, and I want to do something about it while I still can.

I want to pack up Trish, Muffy, Susan, Gary and my grandson, Jacob, and take them to Hawaii for a few days to warm up. I talked to my hospice nurse and the head hospice physician early this week about this and they have given me a big OK.

They figure there is enough strength in these tired old bones and enough capacity in my shrunken lungs for a little R&R in the islands. I also spoke to them about maybe following my heart back to France one more time for Paris in the spring. That's on hold, though.

Rocky Editor John Temple is on board, too, so long as I take along a laptop to keep you posted on my diary. Are you OK with all of this, too? Lordy, I hope so.

Birds big part of magic at old KVOD

Seriously.

I love it when that little "Write" icon pops up in the left corner of my screen. It means I can just let my personal thoughts make their way into my fingers and onto my diary. I was thinking today what a good life this has been, so far at least.

And thanks to hospice I am comfortable and at ease. That was the case when Charley and Jocko Samson and Steve Blatt showed up on my front porch to pass the time of day. I have always liked these guys. We all worked together at the old KVOD and were able to laugh at each other and not take broadcasting classical music too seriously.

That was the trick, the reason our station became so popular. Sure, we took the music seriously but not each other. I'll never forget the day the program director from a large FM station in the East came out to find out what our secret was.

He was a nice little guy with a very serious, profound voice. He identified himself as program director and chief announcer for this station. When he showed up, I was out beside the station feeding the birds underneath our suspended microphone.

It was a hot day and sweat was pouring down my face and onto my ragged T-shirt. I was wearing jeans and kletter boots. When I came in out of the heat, our receptionist introduced me to him.

He said he had noticed how our station had such high audience ratings, and he wanted to study our operation to see if we were doing something his station might be able to use to improve its audience ratings.

I could tell he was somewhat put off by my appearance. I was not at all what he expected as a station owner. "First of all," I began to say, "we don't take this s--t too seriously."

The color drained from the poor guy's face, and he began to stammer in that wonderful, deep, radio voice. I interrupted and told him how we let the birds chirp away during our announcements and commercials and how the audience seemed to love them, and how we were using about 100 pounds of birdseed a week, and how this presented us with something of a bird poo problem, but we didn't care because we loved the birds.

The program director/chief announcer excused himself and backed out of the door to call a cab to take him to the airport. I never heard from him again. Jennifer Gavin, daughter of *Denver Post* columnist Nosmo King, wrote a feature about that incident when she was employed by the Associated Press, and it was widely printed by newspapers around the nation.

It was never published here, however. I don't know why not. I am telling you the story because it sort of explains the spirit we had in the old KVOD and why I was so pleased to have a visit from Steve and the Samsons.

Need I add that we were not begging for money around the clock and trying to get folks to put us in their wills and donate their old station wagons to us.

Yes, it was a good day that ended with my polishing off an original Yoplait after a wonderful steak dinner Trish fixed for us. The Yoplait was key lime pie flavor, and damned if it didn't taste like key lime pie. Cheers to Yoplait! And cheers to the old KVOD folks who came to see me!

February 5

What is Oprah's magazine doing in a barber shop?

OVERNIGHT.

I had forgotten not to try to get a haircut on Saturday. Tom & Jake's shop was jammed with old guys and little kids. Tom wrote my name on the list when I entered. I figured my son, Jon, and I would have time for a haircut and maybe time to cruise by our old house in north Denver to see the garage Brett had put up.

No way. I passed the time waiting by reading the February issue of *O, The Oprah Magazine*. Oprah is on the cover, of course, dressed in red. On the back is a black-and-white photograph of a man kissing a woman on her stomach. It's an advertisement for Ralph Lauren's Romance, a women's fragrance. Ralph somehow missed appearing in the photo shoot. That wasn't like him.

I had always wanted to write a column about *O* and briefly considered taking the magazine home with me, but that would have been stealing, even though I couldn't figure out what *O* was doing in Tom & Jake's barber shop. While waiting for my haircut, I tried memorizing stuff about which I would write.

It didn't work. My memory is shot. It wasn't wasted effort, though. Sensing my constant preoccupation with this chore, Trish had purchased a copy. Of the 16 members of the *O* production staff, only one was a man, Peter Davis, who is research manager. What does that tell us?

Oprah has become a major figure in the publishing world, and authors who want to make *The New York Times* Top 10 had better cozy up to her. I was pleased, however, to note that TV actor Marg Helgenberger is featured with books that have made a difference in her life.

They are: *Madame Bovary* by Gustave Flaubert; *The Poisonwood Bible* by Barbara Kingsolver; *All Quiet on the Western Front* by Erich Maria Remarque; *Notes from the Underground* by Fyodor Dostoevsky; *The Grapes of Wrath* by John Steinbeck; and *The Liar's Club* by Mary Karr.

You know what I think about that? I don't think I have ever read a book that changed my life. I suppose if a big shot like Oprah asked me that question, I would root around through old books I had read and give her a list that would impress her.

Getting back to Marg Helgenberger, I like it that she is from Nebraska and I like her portrayal of a crime investigator in *CSI*, a surprise hit on CBS last year and this. She is not your usual leggy blonde but someone who appears to have been around the block a few times. Her choice of books is admirable, but I wish she had steered clear of enthusiastic modifiers like "incredibly satisfying," "tragic gruesomeness," "unbelievably ambitious" and that kind of thing.

I get the idea that when folks try to write for big magazines, they try too hard. I remember what Greg Pearson used to tell journalism writing classes at Metro State. His advice my daughter remembers best is "accuracy, accuracy, accuracy." Mine from Greg was to "not let too much washing hang from the line," meaning don't clutter your copy with a lot of useless modifiers.

The best advice is write to express, not to impress, but you have heard that warning from me many times before. The magazine has become an overnight success.

She is publishing a magazine on how to live, and I am just an old guy writing a diary on how to die, which we are all going to do, even Oprah.

February 6

Phooey on NFL's commercial hooey

CRANKY.

Enough, already. Folks are making too much of the New England Patriots 20–17 win over the St. Louis Rams in the Super Bowl. (You'll never know how close I came to writing Los Angeles Rams instead of St. Louis Rams. God knows where they will be playing next year.)

Anyhow, does the Patriots' win somehow make the St. Louis Rams unpatriotic? You would think so to hear some folks lavishing praise on New England. Gee, it was just a football game, not a test of loyalty to God and country.

I thought the pregame and halftime televised patriotic hoopla was clearly over the top. Here we had U-2, an Irish band, and English rock star Paul McCartney, winding up to bring lumps to our throats over our devotion to America.

A guy who e-mails me with the pen name of Socoolnow, wrote to me just as the game was starting, "Patriots by 30. Take it to the bank." Well, I didn't take it to the bank, but he clearly had the right team.

I figured the Rams would win big, so I didn't pay too much attention to the game at first. My son, Jon, had borrowed my little Panasonic TV I keep in my office because it gets such a nice picture.

When it became clear the Pats weren't rolling over, I started watching the game in our family room with Trish, and I gave it my full attention deep in the fourth period. I sort of wanted New England to beat the Rams because the Patriots were one of the teams from the old AFL, from which our beloved Bronocs had sprung.

And, in life, I have always come down on the side of the underdogs, which the Patriots clearly were by a couple of touchdowns at least.

Frankly, I thought it was a little tacky when they rolled names of 9–11 victims during the halftime folderol. Had I been a relative of one of those victims, I would have cringed at their names being used in such a commercial way.

Are our perspectives getting a little out of whack, or am I just a cranky old man who can't keep up to date? Do you get the feeling we are all being used all the time for someone else's commercial purpose?

I hate being used, and it seems to me, we are all being used every day without our permission. I surely don't believe that the relatives of any of those 9–11 victims were ever asked if it was OK for the National Football League to exploit them for purely commercial purpose on television, to be seen around the world over and over again.

Does that bother you as it does me? Just playing the national anthem and hiring a bunch of pretty girls to march around waving flags doesn't make it OK. Again, this was just a football game played by a bunch of millionaires to make more millionaires more money.

Look, I'm for making money, as much as I can, but I'll be damned if I want to make it by exploiting others without their permission. So let's get real here.

Congratulations to the Patriots. They won fair and square. I am sure the Rams will be back next year.

Hooray for America. That comes from the heart. But if it comes from the hucksters who are using our patriotism to sell their products, that's a bunch of hooey. I know it, they know it, you know it. Hooey may sell to some people, but hooey doesn't sell to me.

February 7

Goodbyes, yes, but first a little traveling music

GOOD DEATH.

Some folks have talked of my plans to take my family to Hawaii. If I am getting ready to die, how come I am also making plans to go to France after that? What's the deal, anyhow?

My friend Chuck Green has also taken note in *The Denver Post* that I am writing columns every day instead of three a week, as is the custom of personal commentary writers at most newspapers. Where am I getting all this energy?

I don't know. It just seems to be bubbling to the surface. I guess there is just a lot of stuff I want to say before I die. I'll admit it isn't really important. It's just stuff I want to say before I go.

For instance, when I checked out our obituary page, I missed my mother so much. She isn't here to tell me things I ought to know about June Harraway, who died Jan. 28. June was the wife of former *Denver Post* sportswriter Frank Harraway.

With Mike McPhee's help last night, I tried to reach him to convey my heartfelt feelings on her passing. She and my mother were friends, brought together as fans of the old Denver Bears Baseball Club.

I also tried without success to reach Jim Burris, who managed the club until it was phased out of existence by the arrival of our last-place Major League Colorado Rockies. I mention this, not out of anger, but out of affection for minor league baseball that drew us together as friends and lovers of the sport.

I have no idea how many baseball games Frank Harraway scored. But while he was up in the press box deciding the difference between a passed ball and a wild pitch, and up there forever determining which goofs were errors and which were not, my mother was sitting next to June helping her keep score.

The eras seem to end in agate print on the obituary page, and few people seem to give a damn. I care, though, and I am sorry Frank will have to live out the rest of his life without his beloved June.

So why Hawaii? So I can stick my old face in the trade winds again. So I can hear that corn-ball Hawaiian music again. So I can sip a mai tai in the late afternoon as the sun paints the horizon in shades of purple and orange.

So I can watch the whales spout their fountains in the bay off Lahaina.

I want to remember these lines from Shakespeare's *The Merchant of Venice:*

"How sweet the moonlight sleeps upon this bank! Here will we sit, and let the sounds of music creep in our ears: soft stillness and the night become the touches of sweet harmony."

You see? I want to die the good death. Isn't that OK?

In Paris, I won't sleep under Pont Neuf as I did all those years ago when the shooting was over and I went AWOL with two other guys. I will go up to Montmartre, however, to see if Mere Catherine's bistro is still there.

I want Trish to wheel me in my wheelchair along the Left Bank to see if the artists and poets are still there. I want to go again to the Isle de la Cite to marvel at that wonderful old jewel of a city.

DIA in trouble? I would say I told you so, but …

Buh, Bye!

Do you mind if I have a private little snicker over Denver International Airport's municipal bond problems? If not that, maybe a little Mona Lisa smile?

Come on now, as DIA's No. 1 media scold, don't I deserve a tiny bit of recognition now that 18 major international banks have declined to provide the airport with a letter of credit backing $52 million in existing bonds?

The only reason I am not clicking my heels and hollering "I told you so" is that there is a remote possibility that a wee bit of those bonds may be squirreled away in a fund I own.

Lordy, I hope not, Jennifer, if you're reading this. Jennifer Elmore is my financial adviser who keeps me from squandering my ill-gotten gains on nutty get-rich easy schemes.

Let me remind you that when former Mayor Federico Pena, Richard C.D. Fleming and that Greater Denver Chamber of Commerce crowd floated this plan to build DIA, I wondered out loud why we didn't just expand Stapleton Airport onto Rocky Mountain Arsenal land instead.

Of course this would have denied investment bankers money they would have earned on bond sales. And of course scads of money was spent on DIA construction.

We would have saved a bunch of money and kept the airport near town so it would be more accessible. It would cost us less to get there, and our airline tickets would cost less because we wouldn't have to be helping United pay for Tent City out there on the Plains where the deer and the antelope used to play.

Do you remember how we made a deal with United Airlines that it would monopolize air travel in Denver, forcing other airlines either to leave or go into bankruptcy? We all chuckled when United became the 800-pound gorilla at DIA.

There is no point now or space here to go into United's problems with our automated baggage system that made us the laughingstock of the industry. Remember all those funny TV news videotapes showing baggage being thrown every which way?

Now with United facing bankruptcy (I hate that word), it might have to cut back on payments to DIA. And with less income, our beautiful DIA might have to refinance bonds at a higher interest rate. Oh, my goodness!

All of this is happening just as I am getting ready to pack off most of my family, first class, up front, in United Airlines service to Hawaii. I am going to burn off some of my alleged riches to help United in its hour of need and also to give my family a taste of the bubbly before I die.

I suppose, in some small way, I shall be helping DIA avoid the consequences of a possible United bankruptcy. I doubt my largesse will do much to put our Humpty Dumpty baggage system together again, though.

At the moment, it is not clear whether DIA's financial difficulties will affect its $300 million expansion project. You know what can happen to the right hand when the left hand doesn't know what it is doing.

I do hope they can all work it out before we leave. We are all getting packed and ready to go and have learned to say "buh, bye" to the flight attendants when we get there.

February 9

This superb jazz is to die (a little) for

ROMANCE.

It's 11 p.m. Trish and I returned from the Burnsley about an hour ago. She has gone to bed, and I want to write this before my bedtime morphine kicks in. Just as we pulled out of the Burnsley's parking garage, I saw a huge stretch limousine, as my father would say, longer than a bell cord on a picnic train.

I don't know who was in it, but I am sure they didn't have anything that approached the good time we had listening to Ellyn Rucker. It was Dr. Ray Garrett's idea. He is the nephrologist I met months ago at the Swedish Hospital Infusion Center where technicians were trying to save my life by pumping iron into me.

It wasn't working. Not their fault. My red corpuscle count was continuing to diminish. It was in that little room I decided to quit fighting a losing battle for my life. Ray listened quietly to me without comment. He has quit being my physician and has started being my friend.

That's how our relationship began. It has continued on the basis of our mutual love of jazz. He is a big African-American man, really big, towering big. Maybe that's what makes him so soft-spoken. He doesn't use his size to intimidate. He speaks just above a whisper.

In talking to him, we discovered we were both acquainted with that superbly gifted pianist and vocalist, Ellyn Rucker. I have known her longer, perhaps, since those days years ago when I journeyed to the top of old Lookout Mountain to hear her play and sing at Vern Byers' Robin's Nest.

It had been a long time since I had seen her, though, the most recently at a Denver Press Club luncheon. John Ensslin set up a celebrity series to save the poor old Press Club from financial extinction. He is truly a saint for trying to do this.

Ellyn and I have been in contact recently about her plans to promote memorial concerts here and at Boulder to honor her dear friend and great tenor saxophonist, Spike Robinson. It appears now those concerts will take place the week of April 9.

I desperately want to live that long. But let's get back to tonight. Ellyn kept stealing my heart over and over again as she sat alone at the piano singing, "The Folks Who Live on the Hill," "I've Got You under My Skin," "You'd Be So Nice to Come Home To" and "Baby, Ain't I Good to You?"

She really wiped me out, though, and Ray, too, with "Every Time I Say Goodbye I Die A Little." Wow, when she sings that to an old guy who really is dying a little, I just had to hit my chest with my fist for air. You know what I mean by that?

I wish I could have stayed longer, but I was beginning to fog out, and I couldn't hear too well because one of my hearing aid batteries pooped out. Anyhow, it was a wonderful evening for Trish and for me. Trish looked so nice on our "date." She said to me in whispers while Ellyn was playing, "I didn't think people did this sort of thing anymore since the 1970s."

I think the morphine is kicking in now, but the evening did remind me of those wonderful days when I was young and went to places like the Burnsley and felt romance in the air. Gee, I want to do it again, to hear Ellyn again, to feel romance again.

Ellyn, there is no one better than you, now or ever.

February 13

Of reptiles, Olympic judging

SNAKES ALIVE.

Folks seem to be wondering what to do with that 11-foot female Burmese python that wrapped her coils around her owner, Richard L. Barber, 43, strangling him in Aurora Sunday. My first thought would be a nice handbag and pumps to match.

Not only did the snake kill Barber, but she almost crushed Aurora firefighter Sigfried Klein, 29. The snake's name is Monty.

Cheryl Conway, spokeswoman for the Aurora Animal Care Division, said the python will be cared for at the city animal shelter until officials decide what to do with it. She said it is illegal to keep a snake that size in Aurora or anywhere in Colorado, with the exception of a zoo.

I don't know what the shelter will feed Monty, maybe an occasional bunny? I don't even want to think about that.

Many years ago there was a story about a cobra on the loose in Denver. It happened about the same time pedestrian walk lights were being installed downtown. I facetiously suggested maybe slither lights should be added, as well. People who were fearful of snakes didn't think it was funny.

I don't think snakes are funny, either. I have always wondered what Adam was thinking when he let that snake under the tree of knowledge convince him it was OK to take a bite out of the apple. We'll never know. I would have gone for the banana for its potassium content.

Back in 1941 when I was barely able to hang on during my freshman year at the University of Colorado, there was a kid in our dormitory who was deathly fearful of snakes. When the word got out, some of his cruel freshman classmates rounded up all the water and garden snakes they could find down by the creek and put them in the kid's room.

When the poor guy opened his door, they were slithering all over the place. He turned and ran and never came back. I have no idea what happened either to him or his tormentors.

As far as I am concerned, snakes are sort of like the Winter Olympics. I can either take them or leave them. Not so with Trish. She has been glued to the TV since the Games began.

At least she was until Monday night when Olympic judges awarded the gold medal in pairs skating to the Russians by a vote of 5 to 4 instead of the Canadians who were clearly the best skaters.

"I'm never going to watch the Olympics again!" Trish shouted at the TV. It's my bet she will, though. For reasons I don't understand, she is really hooked by the Games this year.

"Come, sit and watch it with me," she says. "I always watch that dumb Super Bowl with you."

Frankly, I thought the American skaters should have won. When American figure skater Kyoko Ina jumped up and planted her ice skates within inches of pair partner John Zimmerman's groin, I would have given the poor guy the gold straightaway.

February 15

I richly enjoyed my News4 cameo

STINGRAY.

I just watched a videotape of an interview Bill Stuart did of me for News4 a few weeks ago. I tried to call him tonight to thank him, but I was never able to hack my way through News4's voice mail system.

Instead, I left a message with Aimee Sporer. I knew her phone number because she is a friend of long standing. She was an intern at the old KVOD before she went into television. What a lovely person she is!

Anyhow, I liked the interview. It showed me just as I am. Trish was pleased with the way our house looked, and, of course, I liked the shot in our garage where I was showing Bill my '67 Stingray. I shall never again unleash those 425 horses under the hood. Bill seemed to enjoy it when I popped the hood. It's a guy thing.

I told Bill I was ready to die anytime. I hasten to add that the interview was done before I decided to take my family to Hawaii. Given my druthers, I'd druther the good Lord would wait until we get back. I also want to take Trish to Paris one more time.

Without much luck, I have tried to explain to my friends about April in Paris, one more time, as Ella and Count Basie put it so eloquently, but I don't think my friends understand. I must have left part of me there all those years ago right after the war.

I don't know if I left it at Mere Catherine's bistro in Montmartre, at Place Pigalle (Pig Alley, as we called it), somewhere on the Left Bank, under Pont Neuf, where two other guys and I slept in our f--t sacks to dodge the snow drops (better known as the MPs), at Notre Dame where hideous gargoyles looked down at us, at the Louvre, or L'Orangerie where all those magnificent impressionist paintings are on display, or … hell, I don't know, but it is over there somewhere, and I would like to try again to find it.

This isn't the column I intended to write today. I wrote one this morning and spiked it this afternoon. It was wretched, awful. I feel as though I have cheated the *Rocky* if I don't crank out a column every day. That's what Pocky Marranzino and Lee Casey did before I came along.

All you do is sit down at the typewriter (the way it used to be), or the computer (the way it is now) and empty your mind through your fingers. What's the big deal? Don't remind me about quality, the kind of quality my friend Tom Gavin practiced here and at *The Denver Post* for so many years. And don't forget Bill Gallo, real wordsmiths, those guys. They're rare practitioners, and my name doesn't even belong in the same paragraph.

Anyhow, I'm ready to die and get out of the way for the next guy to come to the plate, but only after Hawaii and then Paris, where I shall have a brandy Alexander. I don't give a hoot what the doctors say.

I dearly love my family and friends and shall miss all of them if, after death, one is able to miss anyone or anything. As I have written before, it's an open question what's out there.

I loved being on News4 with Bill Stuart, Aimee Sporer and Larry Green. They are my kind of people, and I am flattered they would want me to share time and space with them.

End of column. Good morning!

February 16

I'll send e-postcards from Hawaii

FISTFUL.

Have they gone now? Can we talk? I'm in Dutch because I'm taking along a laptop computer to Hawaii so I can write columns. In unison, Trish and my hospice nurse said, "This is supposed to be a vacation!"

I was surprised Trish had read my column. I've always said that if there's something I don't want her to know, I should write it in my column, because she'll never see it there.

The hospice nurse is reading all my stuff now to keep tabs on my death-and-dying diary. Anyhow, my secret is out, and I have to deal with it. Writing this column isn't work to me. It never has been.

My friend Dick Kreck sent me a nice World War II story, I guess because there are no WWII vets left at *The Denver Post*, where he labors. He underlined my everyday work.

Shucks, folks, it ain't nothin', because I love doing this. *Rocky* editor, president and all that jazz John Temple says it's OK to take off a few days occasionally, and I may do that later, but not now. You only get to die once, and I'm trying to make the best of it.

To Trish and my nurse, it looks as if I'm working when I'm sitting here hammering out this stuff, but I'm not. I'm just emptying my brain. That's what I'll be doing in Maui while the whales are spouting. And, hey, I write fast, even at my age. Ask Ann Carnahan, who sat next to me in the *Rocky* newsroom. I sit down and 30 minutes later I'm outta here, OK?

Something else: To my daughters and Trish, a vacation means going shopping. I hate shopping. What am I supposed to be doing while they plow through acres of muumuus and other Polynesian stuff at Panama Hatties?

Better I should be back at the condo massaging the keys on the laptop. With all the medication I'm taking, I can't be down at the bar inhaling mai tais. I can barely walk and am a lousy swimmer. So, what's left? Just you and me and the laptop, OK?

Sure, I may whip up my famous Northside meatballs for the family. Gary is going to do his beef burgundy for Jacob. We'll have a great time.

I had to apply for my birth certificate for my insurance in case I should kick over before we get back. I ordered five copies. You can never have too many copies of your birth certificate or death certificate.

I learned that when my mother died. Everyone wanted a death certificate, not a photocopy but an original. We just went through this when Trish's father died recently. The survivor designated to handle who gets what needs a fistful of death certificates. Write that down somewhere. You'll thank me for reminding you.

I need a birth certificate to get a passport if we go to France. I threw mine away, figuring I'd never go anywhere anymore. But if Hawaii works out OK, maybe it will be Paris in the spring.

Wow, wouldn't that be something!

February 18

My soul, accessories, ready for trip to paradise

Loosey-goosey.

Trish just came home with a big box of Winchell's glazed donuts. Sticky. I asked her if she ever has coffee while she's waiting for them. She said she doesn't because having coffee at Winchell's is a guy thing: Men smoke cigarettes and talk football.

Anyhow, she brought an apple fritter home for herself. She can eat it here where there are no guys talking football or smoking cigarettes. I sort of doubt Winchell's permits smoking, anyhow.

It is pretty exciting around here as we get ready for our trip to Hawaii. Trish is poring over the L.L. Bean catalog to get me properly attired for our vacation. She's ordering me cargo pants, tropical shirts and a bucket hat.

I have no idea how I shall look in that get-up. It has been a year since I knew I was on death's door and haven't worn anything but sweats. My legs are toothpick skinny. I am afraid folks will laugh when they see me on the beach.

They'll just have to laugh. I have been going up and down stairs all morning. My advice to you is don't live in a house with 28 stair steps. If your lungs are shot, as mine are, you'll have to be on oxygen and have a 50-foot tube trailing behind you.

I am afraid I'll trip over the fool thing and break my hip. That is a no-no at my age and in my condition. That would be rotten the day before we are scheduled to leave, wouldn't it?

And so I am being extra careful walking, taking showers and doing everyday stuff most folks do all the time without much thought. Trish is stocking me up on baby shampoo, baby body wash, tooth paste, Listerine and products like these that old folks find handy.

Last night a nice looking guy came to the door. He introduced himself as Pastor James H. Diehl. Right away, I put my guard up. Preachers keep trying to save my soul even though I don't think it's at risk. My old friend, Ed Scott, from TV days, keeps throwing messages over my transom, trying to scare me into believing in Jesus by threatening me with hell fire that will burn me to a crisp.

Somehow he has the idea I'm not a believer. Pastor Diehl was real low key, which I appreciated. He and I have lived across the street from each other for nine years and had never met. Isn't that strange? He is out of town a lot, though, as a traveling missionary. I'll read the pamphlet he left me on "Don't Die Too Soon," and I suspect that will end it, even though our friendship may continue.

I had a nice talk on the telephone with John Temple last night. He is enthusiastic about stuff I shall write in my diary concerning death and dying in paradise, if that's the way the wind blows.

I am glad folks are loosey-goosey about our family's adventure. I don't want anyone to be up tight. My physician, Dr. Jeanne Day Seibert, and the hospice head doctor and my hospice nurse are all on board with this. I haven't identified my hospice nurse or doctor because they don't want me to. It's some kind of rule.

If I die in Hawaii, that's OK. I can be cremated there and my ashes interred in a military cemetery there, and Trish can bring the American flag back home. Or we can work out details with John Horan at Horan & McConaty to return the ashes to Denver for interment at Fort Logan. What's to worry about?

I'm almost ready. Hey Muffy, don't forget the laptop!

February 20

Frowning at the darn phone is a gift I prefer to keep

IMMORTALITY.

Ring, ring, ring. That's all the phone has been doing all day. Sometimes I hate call-waiting. Folks get irritated when you can't speak to them right away and they keep calling and calling and calling. You know what I mean?

Trish says I ought to take the phone off the hook, but there are some calls I need to receive. It will be so nice when we get to Hawaii and the phone stops ringing.

While I was trying to cope with all the phone calls, CNN was in the background doing a story on life extension. I guess there is some kind of life extension institute to help folks seeking immortality.

It involves organ transplant and cosmetic surgery to help old folks look younger. There is some kind of medical procedure that can put a perpetually pleased look on your kisser in much the same way morticians do to dead folks.

The problem is that you can never change expression when you need to. You can't frown. You can't look p---ed off. You can't look elated when you win the lottery. I don't know about that.

This whole business of wanting to live forever baffles me. Life is a wonderful gift, but even the nicest gifts don't last forever. Something else; if we all become immortal, this old planet will become a pretty crowded place.

I'm getting ready to die, and I am looking forward to it as an adventure I haven't had. And I certainly don't want my face pumped full of some kind of gel to make me look like a 42-year-old guy who can only smile.

I didn't know it was so difficult to get touring companies to take money. Without thinking, I gave my daughter, Muffy, my two credit cards to pay for our air fare to the islands. I woke up in the middle of last night realizing those cards would be maxed out, and we wouldn't be able to order cargo pants for me from L.L. Bean.

I called Muffy away from her job this morning to explain the problem. She said the tour company would need some kind of electronic transfer of funds from my bank to her bank from which American Express will access funds for our tickets.

Man, oh man, did I ever run into a bunch of gobbledygook over that.

Finally, a nice young woman just suggested I write Muffy a check and deposit it in her account. That's what I am trying to do now. Somehow, I doubt this will work even though the funds are available in my bank and it is less than a mile to her bank. I'm waiting to find out. I like to think of this as a real-time diary page.

To calm my nerves, I am eating an Original Yoplait 99% Fat-Free Tropical Fruit Yogurt to get me in the mood for Hawaii. Under the foil lid it said, "Please Play Again." I didn't know I was playing anything.

It sort of reminded me of the Smoozie we bought in junior high school that sometimes offered a freebie on the stick when you licked it off. I keep licking off the stick on my chocolate-covered vanilla ice cream Dove bars hoping the same thing is true, but it isn't.

Yoplait wants me to try again to win a trip to Athens for the 2004 Olympics. Sorry, I won't be around for that. Whoops! The phone just rang. I hope its good news.

It was Muffy. The funds transfer is now complete, and there is nothing to worry about. Our tickets are paid for, and my credit cards aren't maxed out so I can get my cargo pants from L.L. Bean that will make my skinny legs look funny.

Quote: "What hath God wrought?"—Samuel F. B. Morse.

February 22

I've chowed down on dog, but never knowingly

SINGSONG.

Before I opened my eyes this morning, I wondered what in the heck I would write about today. Public Radio answered my question with a piece they were doing about a dust-up over President Bush's visit to South Korea.

No, it didn't concern his hard-line comments about North Korea being part of an Evil Axis. It was about what to serve the American president at a state dinner. Some wanted to serve him dog meat, because in South Korea it is considered a delicacy.

No, it doesn't taste like chicken. It's more like pork. I know, because I ate dog meat in South Korea, only I didn't realize it was dog meat until later when some of my fellow war correspondents advised me it was sweet and sour cocker spaniel.

I gagged at that, but it was too late. These guys persuaded me I ought to go to what was called a "singsong" house for a little South Korean entertainment. It was really an imitation of a Japanese geisha house.

I felt ridiculous the whole evening, playing silly games with South Korean girls dressed up in kimonos held together with makeshift obi scarves. We clapped hands and did tricks with chop sticks.

I wanted out of there, but the other guys insisted we have dinner first. The food was sort of spare, but the nation was at war, and I hadn't expected much. When the meat course was served, it was on small bones and in a sweet and sour sauce. I just assumed it was pork. I ate it all. It was OK.

I have always been a truth seeker, but I could have done without learning that truth. When the subject of dog meat comes up, I can't imagine myself eating my dear old Oreo, or Yazzie, or Snoop, or Daisy, or Mr. Chips, or Baron, or any of the other animal companions who have enriched my life. Notice I refer to them as who, not that, because I think of them as human personalities.

South Korea is surely not the way I remember it during the Korean War when we were billeted at the Naija Apartments. It was one of the few buildings in Seoul left standing after the North Korean occupation.

It had one outhouse serving all of us, except "all of us" included a single female correspondent, Mae Craig of the Gannett newspapers. You remember her. She was that lovely middle-age lady in a pillbox hat who later bedeviled President Kennedy at his news conferences. He loved sparring with her, though, calling her "Miss Mae," in a very courtly way.

Let me tell you, she was one tough lady. She crawled on her belly with Marines on patrol. She went on jet strikes along the Yalu. There was absolutely nothing this old gal wouldn't do to get a story. She always did it in such a classy way.

Anyhow, it was a great day of celebration when a second outhouse was constructed for her benefit. Because of my broadcast experience, I was selected to make a speech and present her with a giant wooden key to unlock the door. A wonderful photo was taken of the event by a shooter for the old *Saturday Evening Post.* I would give almost anything today to have a copy of it, but I suppose that is impossible. I, too, loved Miss Mae, as we all did.

I suppose there will always be something to write about when I open my eyes.

Old Tom Gavin once told me always to keep my eyes and ears open and something would be there.

Nothing chases the blues away like kind words

FORLORN.

When I awakened with the blues this morning, I started sorting out my snail-mail. The kindness of so many people brings me around. I have it in four large FedEx boxes which Michelle Quintana uses to forward my mail to me.

I three-hole punch my e-mail messages and have them sorted out by date (kind of) in six 2-inch ring binders. I am trying to read everything sent to me, even a few "get well" cards.

Speaking of that, I am trying to make the best of what life I have left. Sure, I am dying, but I am trying to squeeze the most out of what's left of me. That's why in the morning I do 100 waist bends and as many knee bends as I can, which is not many.

Angie Aufdemberge, my personal trainer, comes to my house once a week to train me on my BowFlex. She sets up the equipment to all she believes I can comfortably and safely handle at my age and in my condition. Look, I'm 78, and I tire easily.

She is a certified trainer as well as a certified massage therapist. After my BowFlex training, she gives me massage therapy on my neck, back and legs, which are very thin.

What I am trying to do is be in the best shape I can when we go to Hawaii. I'm taking most of my family along because I want to be with them as long as I can, and I want to watch Jacob, my 5-year-old grandson, run and play in the surf.

I had to feel sorry for Hospice of Metro Denver. Someone accused them of fraud because they will be arranging for my care in Hawaii. Hospice is not paying for my trip. I am. It's costing me a bundle. They supply me with oxygen there as here.

It's money I have squirreled away over the years by moonlighting at the *Rocky* while still working at the radio station. It's money from my *Rocky* pension. It's money I saved from my Social Security. It's money I put away when Ed and I sold our radio station.

I'm a frugal old guy, and I am paying for the trip, not Hospice. I want to do this for my family. They have all been good to me, and I want to do this for them before I die because I love them. I hope this clears up this foolish fraud charge, OK?

I have run out of pizzelle cookies, though, and my son, Jon, will take me out to Jim Garramone's store tomorrow to get some more. I ate all the ones he and his wife sent me. I also ate all the pizzelles Dorothy Pastore sent me as I did the pizzelles Rose Maroney baked for me. By the way, Dorothy is 90 years old, bless her heart.

You see how it makes me feel better to read my mail? I was particularly pleased to hear from the Borscht Brothers, whom I heard at that wonderful West Colfax Jewish reunion I attended some years back. They are Bruce Geller and Jay Halpern, who also sent me a CD of their music.

I just love reading our newspaper, even though it makes me wish I had started out as a sports writer. Did you read Bernie Lincicome's column about Picabo Street's last downhill race at the Olympics? My God, I could sit here at this computer for what's left of my life and not write a column like that. It was superb.

And Dave Krieger, what about him? He is the perfect sports columnist. I have to say though, that I miss his coverage of those forlorn Nuggets when they were coached by Doug Moe. Wasn't he a piece of work?

Reading our newspaper helps me get rid of the blues.

February 26

My wheelchair's a no-show, but we made it to blue Maui

SKITTERING.

We're here, and everything is OK. Almost. So we lost my wheelchair. It must be somewhere at Los Angeles International Airport, where we had only 20 minutes to change planes from our Denver flight to our plane to take us to Maui. I hopped onto a chair with my name on it, and the little UAL ticket agent whizzed me at breakneck speed to the Maui check-in counter.

We made it with no seconds to spare.

Leaving Denver, I was pleased to hear Reynelda Muse's and Pete Smythe's recorded voices on the DIA train. Of course, Pete is dead and

Rey is living in Indianapolis. I saw her here in Maui on HGTV. Her snow-white hair contrasted against her ebony skin was stunning.

United baggage guys somehow transferred our bags to the Maui flight on time. I guess my wheelchair got lost in the scramble, but they'll find it, I'm sure. I have to say, the United people have been great, so far.

OK, so we were sitting up in the pricey section. I told my family we were going first class, and I am paying for everything—that means everything. I have saved my money for this trip, and I want it to be nice for them. That's my way of enjoying this vacation.

Getting back to United's service, it has really been superb. I used to think the term "airline food" was an oxymoron, like "military intelligence" or "rush-hour traffic," but I have to say the ravioli United served me for lunch yesterday was the best I have ever eaten. Award-winning chefs should live so long. Wow!

Right now, I am figuring out Muffy's laptop, upon which I am trying to scratch out this diary page. The family is down on the beach watching Jacob play in the surf. I am not doing too well on this fool thing. The cursor keeps skittering up to the top of the page, screwing up what I have already written.

It's a lot more high-tech than my Gateway desk-top at home, but Muffy promises me I shall get the hang of it. So far, though, it has been hunt-and-peck all the way. She tells me I had better hit the "save" button all the time, so I better do it now. It worked, I guess.

Something else: I can't seem to find the delete button. She showed me, but she is down at the beach with Jacob, and I don't want to bother her.

Susan, Gary, Jacob and Muffy went to the grocery store for Gary to fix his beef Burgundy for dinner tonight. Jacob loves it. Susan said they spent $460. Food is very expensive here. That's OK. As I said, I want it to be nice. Susan wants me to fix my Northside meatballs while we're here. That's a "big maybe."

I had to take a quick break for cottage cheese nourishment so I can eat while I work. You should know I am writing this diary page in real time. That means I am not waiting to eat until I finish. I am hungry right now and have to do something about it while I am writing, without splattering cottage cheese all over Muffy's WinBook laptop.

Did I tell you, my esophageal procedure that was done before we left for Maui didn't quite work, and I have to return to the hospital when we get back to Denver for a repeat? I can still force down food by gulping a lot of water.

I try not to think about it by watching morning rainbows bridge across Lahaina Bay, where whitecaps are really white in water that is really blue.

How I love watching tropical birds roller-coaster on cool trade-wind gusts. All the glances out my window are perfect pictures. I wish you could see them as I can. I'll just have to pretend you are here with us.

February 27

Serious questions jarring in rainbow-filled paradise

LEGOS.

Gary's beef burgundy was all Jacob said it would be. I was so stuffed I had to waddle over to my bed to collapse and sleep to the sound of waves smashing on the beach just below my window.

Walking is difficult for me, though. My feet are so swollen, the only footwear I can stand are those funny woven grass shoes I bought here maybe 15 years ago. When I was packing, something told me I ought to bring them with me. Good choice.

United Airlines found my missing wheelchair, and the gang will push me into Whalers Village tonight for dinner. Susan is trying to convince me I should get into the hot tub just outside my window, something that would feel mighty good on my tired old bones and muscles.

No way. I checked it out yesterday, and it was filled with twenty-something chicks in string bikinis and muscle-bound guys flexing their abs and their pecs.

If you think I am going to put my 127-pound bony butt and wrinkled, bruised and scarred body in there with them, you have another think coming. Maybe, though, I could sneak down there at midnight while the twentysomethings are partying elsewhere.

I loved it last night when Jacob took me by the hand to the balcony to watch him assemble a new Legos toy that Gary had purchased for him. Kids his age are crazy about Legos, I guess.

The conversation turned serious. He started pointing at pictures in the catalog and began asking me some tough questions about war. It all started when he wanted to know about cutting off the head of the evil king when the good guys won.

"You were in the war, right, Grandpa?" he asked. I told him I was and tried to explain what we did and what we had to do. It wasn't easy. I hated it that we had to talk of such things in a beautiful place where God manufactures rainbows, and where whales spout such glorious towers of sea water.

He looked at me with those serious blue eyes and said, "Those are interesting questions, aren't they?" I never heard of such a comment coming out of the mouth of a 6-year-old boy, have you?

The folks who own this condominium are an interesting lot. There is a little sign on the table by the front door that says:

"Aloha.

"Welcome to our home. In the Hawaiian tradition, would you please remove your shoes upon entering.

"For smokers, we have provided ashtrays on our beautiful lanai.

"Mahalo."

I didn't see the sign until we had been here for a day, and so we had tramped all over the place without realizing we had violated house rules. Bummer.

At least none of us smokes, so I guess we can put our chewing gum in the ashtrays.

February 28

Even in Maui, the memories drift back to Curtis Street

CURTIS STREET.

What would you say if I were to tell you we are going to spend another week in paradise? That's the drill. We have cleared it with everyone except my boss, John Temple, at the *Rocky*. Is this OK with you, John, or are you going to drag me back kicking and screaming?

The oxygen guys just left after leaving me six bottles of the good stuff.

Add to that all the O$_2$ the Invacare compressor can manufacture for me in my bedroom. Gary just fixed the foot rests on my wheelchair and I am ready to rock and roll all over Maui.

Susan has made reservations for everyone but Trish and me for a helicopter tour of the island. Trish isn't going because choppers scare her. I am not going because I have been there and done that.

Susan also set up a scuba dive for Gary. I tried to talk him into playing golf on one of Maui's great courses. He said he didn't want to be away from his family that long, and besides, he said, there are golf courses in Denver. I told him they are all covered with snow, but he wouldn't budge.

I was so pleased when we arrived to find a greeting card from my old friend, Spero Armatas. He and his cousin, George Bouzarelos, own my favorite southwest Denver eatery, Newbarry's, that still serves folks from a counter.

I love counter service, particularly when Virginia pours my coffee without being told, and the countermen baste eggs just the way you want 'em and serve your breakfast while it is still piping hot. Newbarry's also is one of the few places where you can still get Curtis Street chili the way Sam's No. 3 served it for many years, with vinegar on the side.

I still have these memories even though I am thousands of miles away from old Curtis Street that isn't there anymore.

While Gary is taking a dip with Jacob in the pool, Trish, Muffy and Susan are shopping in Whaler's Village. They think I am at the laptop working, but this isn't work. It's my way of emptying my brain through my fingers. I may let the surf lull me into a little nap time pretty soon, though.

Did I happen to mention to you that my optician, Ralph Donahue, came out to my house before we left to fit me with a new pair of glasses? He brought along another pair he made for me to help me work at a computer. Somehow, he took my regular prescription and morphed it into lenses that focus better on a computer screen.

I called him before I left and told him how happy I am with them. They really are helping me here with the laptop I have borrowed from Muffy. They seem to bring the entire script into focus without my having to move my head all the time. I know this is difficult to understand, but I am explaining it the best I can.

That's all for this time. When Trish returns, she's going to wheel me out along the beach so I can see the setting sun. I really love it here. It is such a glorious place to either live or die.

Memories can be fickle companions

IMPRESSIONIST.

Thank goodness the Winter Olympics are over. Even from here, I couldn't endure any more triple axels or the wild enthusiasm that seems always to accompany them.

My memories of this place are leaving me a little sad. From my window, I see a promontory into the sea on which there appears to be a lofty castle. I remember it from 15 years ago. I was on the other side then, staying in a Mahana condominium with Trish and Susan.

I wakened each morning at dawn, slipped into shorts and T-shirt and jogged along the beach all the way to the castle. It was about a mile. I stop occasionally to catch my breath, but I can run most of the way. I do pretty well for a guy in his sixties. The wet sand feels good squishing through my toes as I run along the beach.

Sitting here alone in my wheelchair now, I can see Jacob building four sand castles. He wonders how long they will last. I have to imagine wet sand squishing between my toes.

My memory is playing tricks on me again. Just last night, I was frantically looking in my wallet for a four-leaf clover my mother gave me in 1942 when I went off to fight the Germans. She said she didn't believe such things bring good luck, but to carry it with me, anyhow.

I kept it all those years, and suddenly it was gone, at least I had thought it was lost. Trish had to remind me I had given it to Jacob just a few days earlier, as a memento of my mother.

I felt so foolish not remembering my gift to Jacob. My memory works OK, though, as I watch him build his four little sand castles.

My memory returns me to 40 years ago, and there I am, standing on a beach at Carmel-by-the-Sea, in California. It is dusk. Muffy, Brett and I are getting ready to return to our little cabin.

Jon stays behind where he had built his four little sand castles. He doesn't want to leave them. Some other children are walking by. He doesn't know them, but I hear him say: "Hey, kid. If you are still here in the morning, see if my sand castles are OK."

Why is it I remember Jon's sand castles from 40 years earlier, but I couldn't remember giving my four-leaf clover to Jacob just a few days ago? I'll have to chalk it up to an old saying I just revised: "Time, tides and sand wait for no man, or for little boys, either."

It came to me last night as Gary pushed my wheelchair along the sea to the Rusty Harpoon for dinner. A light rain was falling and it felt so refreshing on my face as we wheeled along the coast.

The tide reminded me of Claude Debussy's *La Mer*, his impressionist musical tribute to the sea. I hope my memory somehow will let me again feel the freshness of the rain against my face and the sound of the sea on this lovely Maui night.

March 2

Buy gum? By golly, you can't do it here

FUNNIES.

The lady was crawling along the shrubbery under my window. "Are you looking for this bathing suit?" I asked.

"Yes," she said. "Did you happen to find a white nightie, too?"

Trish said, "Is that it in the bush over your head?" The lady grabbed it and made her way out of the shrubbery and told her friends the lost garments had been found. No thank you's, though. California people.

They had been boozing most of the day on pina coladas. All were talking and laughing all at once, and I couldn't understand much of anything they were saying except that they were from California.

Red flags were up all day, and no one was swimming in the wild sea. It was certainly a bad-hair day along most of the Maui coastline.

Even so, it was lovely inland. There is no prettier place on Earth. It's the darnedest thing, though, folks along the beach were talking on cell phones.

Why do they come here if all they are going to do is talk on the telephone? Go figure. By the way, I couldn't find any funnies in *The Honolulu Advertiser*. What kind of newspaper is that?

I wonder if they could use a personal commentary columnist to pep up the paper. Just kidding, boss. I have known guys who couldn't wait to move here. After about a year, though, they were ready for stateside again. Something about island fever.

It's interesting what you can, and can't, get here. I have to have chewing gum all the time to keep my mouth moist. Otherwise the narcotics I take make me so dry I can barely speak.

Muffy and I tried to buy some at the little convenience store here at the Whaler. "No gum," the guy at the counter said.

"You have cigarettes, but no gum," Muffy shot back.

"Can't have gum. It's in the lease," he explained. "They don't want gum in the swimming pool or stuck in the carpets."

I guess that figures. The inconvenience is made up for in Maui by Haagen-Dazs chocolate-covered chocolate ice cream bars. I rate them right up there with Dove dark chocolate-covered vanilla ice cream bars.

On another matter, I am concerned about Trish's knee. It has been very painful for her to walk, or even to stand. When we get home, she'll have to be checked out by one of those orthopedic guys.

The way she describes the pain reminds me of the torn cartilage I had on my left knee some years back. The surgery then was to remove all the cartilage. It was painful, and it took a long time to recover.

It's a different deal now that arthroscopic surgery has been developed. It's a much simpler and less painful procedure. We'll know more when an orthopedic surgeon examines her.

Susan will take me to the bookstore in the morning to buy a dictionary. Looking over this copy reminds me how much I need one.

I can spell luau, though. That's tomorrow night.

March 4

Maui retains much of its old allure and charm

SWAGGED.

Old Lahaina is about the way I remembered it from 15 years ago, except for the sign at the southern edge of town that said, "Jesus Coming Soon." We were a little early, though, when Susan and I picked up Gary after his scuba dive, which he said was sensational.

He swam with the dolphins and listened to whales squealing at each other under water. Susan and Jacob waited for him on the shore.

I sat in the rented Windstar van and listened to Mozart's Third Piano Concerto on Hawaiian public radio. The announcer didn't beg for money, which was nice for a change.

We parked not far from Carol Burnett's old house she owned when she was interested in saving whales. They regularly visit the bay just outside Lahaina. I'm not sure if Carol comes around anymore, though.

Front Road coming in is interesting. There are still squatty old houses that haven't been gobbled up by developers. There's no telling how long they will last, with the determination to build strip malls everywhere.

I did see a broken down Model-T Ford truck sitting behind one of those old shanties and was tempted to ask the owner how much he wanted for it. I could ship it back home to have my son, Jon, restore it.

I think he has his hands full with his '79 Camaro and his '68 Firebird, not to mention his '73 Dodge Charger. What the heck, this is supposed to be a vacation.

I have so enjoyed motoring through old Maui now that the roads are widened some and lined this time of year with crimson bougainvillea.

Flowers everywhere are a riot of color and fragrance. Tonight at the Hyatt Regency Luau, Trish, Muffy and Susan were wearing yellow leis of plumeria with the most seductive aroma imaginable.

As advertised, the luau was "not your average torch song." There was a lot of hammering of drums and flaming torches that introduced the telling of ancient Hawaiian myths. They relate the history of Maui and how it has survived to become a Mecca for Pacific tourism.

As dramatic as the telling was, it couldn't compete with the mounds of delicious Polynesian food that tempted all of us. I had forgotten how absolutely delicious Maui onions are, particularly when they are pickled and served on a bed of rice.

The beef, pork and chicken were all superb surrounded by slices of fresh pineapple and papaya. I stayed away from the poi, though, as I had on my three previous visits to the islands.

I also chickened out on the hula dance instruction. I pledged to Trish I would never again be hauled under protest to the stage in front of others to wiggle my creaky old torso for the amusement of others too swagged on mai tais to do the same.

Kite-flying painting sends me soaring

JUICIEST.

I'm going to miss this bedroom. We are staying a few more days, and so Trish and I will have to move up to the third floor because the owners of this condominium are coming back.

That's OK, because their friends are calling at all hours and are coming to the door looking for them. One old guy in a big straw hat just doesn't want to believe they are not here, and speaks to me as though he thinks I am something of an intruder.

I'll miss this bedroom because of the painting on the wall facing the bed. It's large, about 4 feet by 5 feet. It shows 10 little brown-legged boys flying kites from a grassy bluff overlooking the sea.

If you've followed this column over the years, you know how I adore kites. They send children's imaginations soaring into the sky. Kids pretend they are pilots looking down at the world below. The painting is done with a pallet knife dappling orange sunset colors into Maui's evening sky. The artist's first name is Lee. I can't read his last name because of how he scrawls it.

The kids are dressed in shorts and are standing in knee-high grass. The kites are diamond-shaped, like the High Flyers I remember as a kid. They are blue, red, orange and white, and they have tails probably torn from old bed sheets. Wonderful! The painting sent my imagination to flight, as well.

There is no getting away from Denver. Waiting in the luau line last night, Bradley Lane's father stopped me and wanted me to tell his son back home what a wonderful time he is having. Bradley, of Denver, sent his folks here for relaxation in the sun.

I must say our family is in much better shape than some of the local folks who appear ready for sumo wrestling training. Many are overweight big time, as are tourists from other islands, and even some stateside folks billeted below us. Some, though, stay in shape by power walking.

It is sort of sad to see that sugar cane fields have given way to developers building condominium housing and strip malls for the tourist industry. Same thing for pineapple, papaya and onion farming, all of which Maui has been very proud of in the past.

I suppose it is cheaper to raise pineapples in Mexico and less expensive to ship them to the United States from there than it is from here. Still, though, I like to think Hawaiian pineapples and papaya are the juiciest and best in the world.

One thing I don't miss, though, is the burning of sugar cane stalks after the harvest and the great clouds of black smoke that swept across the horizon. Wind gusts that spank Maui every day keep the air from being polluted, though.

Somehow, all this reminds me of our problems back home. We have such beautiful land that folks want to visit, but when they get here, they want to stay, fouling the environment. There is no solution for that, either here or there, damn it!

March 6
Leonard also deals with his last days

LEONARD.

When Susan told me about him, I thought he might be suffering from Alzheimer's disease. I wanted to talk to him because I am suffering from Newsheimer's disease. At least that is my old pal Suzannne Weiss' diagnosis of my condition.

However, Leonard is a very fragile old guy who is terminally ill with Parkinson's disease, among other ailments. Actually, he is considerably younger than I, but doesn't look it.

He told me he has had several bypass surgical procedures and is being treated for cancer. He pointed to his neck just under his ear, suggesting to my untrained eye that his lymph nodes may be involved.

He complained to me about his pain and his inability to sleep. Leonard says his son sends him to Maui to soak up some sunshine in the hope it will ease his condition.

Since we are both terminally ill, I asked him if he happened to be a hospice patient. He said he is not and didn't seem to know much about it. How sad that is, when he, at least, could be given some comfort care until he dies.

Leonard is from Idaho, where he is a retired dairyman. He has been here for two months, suggesting he and his family are pretty well off.

I didn't want to be pushy about explaining hospice to him, but certainly someone should take him under wing, so to speak.

In the months I have been receiving hospice comfort care, I have found there are so many people who don't know what it is or what it does. Many think hospice is just a place to go and die.

It is true there are hospice residence facilities to take care of terminally ill people who lack home resources. I suspect, however, many hospice patients prefer to die at home. That is my intention.

Leonard and I shall talk again, and maybe—within the bounds of good taste—I can tell him more about an alternative to the kind of care he is now receiving. I have found that there are even many physicians who don't understand what hospice is and does. It's worth a shot.

Meanwhile, I am enjoying myself immensely watching Jacob swim and play with other kids. He can get the Cartoon Network here, and he's OK as long as he can watch Angelica and the rest of the Rugrats gang. I'll tell you one thing, though, I can do without Catdog.

Judging from all the drums, there must have been another luau a couple of hotels down on the beach from here. I could hear a Polynesian spiel over a public address system that must have been like the one we heard the other night that told the history of Maui kings and their sons.

For all the world, it sounded like "Yaka hula hickey dula" to me, but that's only a guess. I'm not fluent in any of the many languages spoken here. I have noticed, though, that "please" and "thank you" translate pretty easily. Folks ought to remember those magic words wherever they are, in Maui or at home.

March 7

Stuck in a room with a view

THRUSH.

It has been an entirely satisfactory afternoon. Trish and I had to move up one flight to Susan and Gary's room for the night. The owners of our condominium are returning tomorrow, and the maids need time to clean up the place.

The view from here is so much more rewarding. I can watch Jacob washing sand from his feet and see Trish soaking up the sun as the tide pounds against the beach. In the distance, I can watch whales spout and dolphins arch into the air. Tomorrow, we move up to the third floor for the final 5 days of our stay here. I think I'll enjoy it even more because I'll be able to see even farther.

I just ate the last of my 3 Haagen-Dazs chocolate-covered-chocolate ice cream bars. It was a rotten trick of the Haagen-Dazs people to put only 3 of their bars into a box for those of us who have become accustomed to 4 Dove bars in a box. I was careful, though, not to splatter chocolate on postcards Trish is sending to her sisters and friends. I certainly wouldn't want to do a thing like that.

I've been reading and rereading Thomas Lynch's superb memoir *The Undertaking—Life Studies From the Dismal Trade*. I can't imagine why God squandered such literary skills on a mortician and left poor fools working in newspapers to struggle and struggle some more. I'm fond of quoting John F. Kennedy at times like this: "Life is unfair," and so is death, I guess. I must get this book for Tom Gavin. It made me weep and laugh and weep again.

How I envy Gary swimming with the dolphins and listening underwater to the whales, and I wish I didn't get so damned seasick and could be on those little sailboats I see playing tag with whitecaps as far as I can see.

Oh well, I guess I should be grateful for what I have and not sorry for what I don't have. Did I mention this has been a glorious afternoon? It has. The air has been so clean, the breeze so cool, the sun so bright, my family so happy.

Leonard has been asking for me down at the pool. He wants one of my business cards so he can get a copy of the *Rocky* to read what I wrote about him. I've never carried business cards in my life, and I don't suppose he's computer-literate and able to find it on our Web site.

I guess I'll just scribble out the *Rocky's* snail-mail address. That ought to get it.

My mouth is getting that damnable thrush infection again. My hospice nurse gave me some stuff to swish in my mouth and swallow. I can't figure out why such a damnable infection should be named after a bird.

A time for a family to reflect— and make new memories

BROODING.

It is afternoon here. Susan, Gary, Jacob, Muffy and Trish are below me on the beach, lounging in the sun. Jacob is playing tag with the waves as they crash into shore.

I want to fill my eyes with him while I can. I realize that is just a figure of speech because I have only one eye left.

My memories are filled with the same scenes of Muffy, Brett, Jon and Susan playing in the surf when they were his age. Now, my grandson has joined them in those same images.

Trish and I spoke again this morning of the heart-pounding beauty of Maui. We talk of it every day. There is no blue in the world as blue as the sea outside my window.

The breeze is cool and enough to keep the palm fronds busy. It pleases me Jacob is having so much fun with Muffy under them. He'll always remember her well.

I wish I could linger in his memory as long as my grandfather has in mine. The chemistry is different, though. Grandpa and I were thrown together by the circumstance of the Great Depression.

I suppose it is fair to say he became my surrogate father at a time when my dad was so depressed by being unemployed that he consoled himself alone. He was in the attic of Grandpa's old house on West Maple brooding about circumstances beyond his control.

And so Grandpa and I went up Broadway together for strawberry ice cream cones and to Merchants' Park for baseball games. Jacob is sharing most of these experiences with his father, as he should. I love watching the closeness of their relationship.

We had a scrumptious dinner last night at the Hula restaurant down the beach. My shrimp scampi was the best I ever tasted. The shrimp were almost as large as lobster tails, and the noodles tasted like homemade, and perhaps they are.

The Hula was too far for me to walk, even dragging my oxygen bottle behind me. Gary had to push me in my wheelchair.

Each time we travel that way, I am reminded of how difficult life is for physically challenged folks everywhere. Is that the politically correct way of describing us?

Most of my life I have looked at folks in wheelchairs with some pity, but usually with a little annoyance.

Now, the shoe is on the other foot, and I am struggling with my infirmity and will continue to do so for the rest of what little life is left for me.

This reminds me of Susan's senior year in high school at Denver's Career Education Center.

As part of her awareness training, she had to spend a week in a wheelchair going to, and coming from school in a bus. We had to lift her in and out of bed and perform tasks for her she couldn't.

It was a great experience for her and for us, and she has never forgotten what life can be for those who have physical impairments. Now, I am learning the same lesson late in my life.

March 9

Paradise is tempting, but it's not home

LEGERDEMAIN.

CNN *Headline News* is prattling on about scattered corpses in Georgia and Catholic priests fondling little boys in Boston, and I am here, wondering why Trish and I have to leave this place.

Trish said to me this morning, "Well, you don't have to go if you don't want to." What she said seems to make sense as I look out the window and see whales spouting and dolphins arching into the sky. After all, how much time do I have left?

There is a lovely mantle of clouds just barely hiding the tip of the mountain about three miles from here. It isn't quite so pretty as the foothills I see from our kitchen window at home, but it will do.

I talked on the telephone with Brett at home for a few minutes last night, and he told me how cold it has been in Denver. It is just shirt-sleeve warm along the beach.

There are no scattered corpses here, and if there are any little boys being fondled, I haven't heard of it. But I shake my head to clear it. Life isn't perfect here, either.

The surf is mesmerizing me and I know there is reality out there beyond the horizon. Much of what I see is illusion, and so we'll be going home as scheduled.

If I were to stay, I couldn't keep Jacob with me. I would miss my daughters; I already miss my sons, Brett and Jon, back home. Also, I would miss the *Rocky*, with which I fell in love years ago.

We went to a magic show and buffet at the next hotel up the beach last night. Standing in line in front of us was a comely girl with skintight pants that barely covered her rear-end decollete.

It revealed the top of a tattoo of what appeared to be the face and wings of either an angel or some kind of wicked personage. I couldn't tell who or which and was too embarrassed to ask.

I was glad when the line finally moved in and we could line up for the buffet and wait for the magic show. The food was delicious, and I pigged out, big-time.

The show began with the usual telling of the story of the God, Pele, and how angry he was at something, I forget. About then, my lungs began to ache, and Muffy had to go back to our condominium for my wheel chair and oxygen bottle.

I missed the last half of the show, and how Gary was taken to the stage for some kind of legerdemain gimmickry. Trish said he was wonderful, even better than his hula demonstration the other night at a luau we all attended.

He was a better sport than I would have been. My cane and wheel chair are a good excuse from my being dragged to the stage for such amateur involvement in every show here.

Hey, it has been a wonderful vacation, and we have 3 more days to enjoy it. I still would like to stay, though.

March 11

Island supermarket also has food for the spirit

SAUCY.

Another wonderful day in paradise. I got to go to Safeway and everything. That may seem like old hat to you, but it has been many months since I have seen the inside of a supermarket.

I made it all the way to checkout without my oxygen bottle. I do much better at sea level than at Mile High, Smile High Denver. There is surely more oxygen here for my pulmonary fibrosis-damaged lungs.

Maybe it is my imagination, but I am convinced that the Invacare machine that compresses regular air for oxygen works better here. I need it to breathe at night and when I am just horsing around in our condominium.

My point is that the oxygen I am breathing is enriched with the sweet air from the sea. That may not scientifically be true, but I want to believe it anyhow. I just love this place!

Safeway was a big treat because there was stuff on the shelves I had not seen before. I guess I was pretty much an impulse shopper because I loaded up our basket.

The trip Susan, Gary and Jacob took to Hana was a disappointment. Even though they had rented a Jeep Wrangler, Jacob became terribly carsick and barfed all over the back seat.

I made that drive alone 15 years ago, and was terrified at every twist and turn in the road. It is difficult to drive because the bridges—and there are hundreds of them—are one-way.

I can compare it to Virginia Canyon back home between Idaho Springs and Central City, or Independence Pass, or Montana's Cook City highway. If you have the stomach for it, the drive to Seven Falls where Charles Lindbergh is buried is worth it.

You drive through jungles and rain forests. The views are spectacular. I saw peacocks spreading their colorful tails along the way. It's really lovely, if your stomach is up to it.

Hawaiians who live there are not friendly to tourists. They blame visitors for stealing their land and corrupting their culture.

Maybe they are right. The folks are friendlier in Lahaina, though. Tonight a sand bucket was waiting for me filled with candy, cookies and gum—which I desperately need to keep my mouth moist because of narcotics I must take.

It was from Saucy Walter, of Eldorado Market, who must read my column on the Internet. Saucy writes: "It's wonderful you have stayed here and cherished your time together in Maui. May the rest of your visit be filled with aloha and wonderful memories."

My morning was filled with glazed doughnuts and macadamia nut cookies. There is no shortage of macadamia nuts here. The honey-roasted are very special.

Tomorrow, Trish is cooking stateside. We are having corned beef and cabbage and oven-browned spuds, which I dearly love.

March 12

Rainbow a lovely parting gift

HIGH-FIVE.

Trish is still asleep. It is morning, and the sea is gray. I see a lonely figure walking along the sandy beach. I wish I were he, but I'll settle for fresh coffee here on the third floor of our condominium.

My fingers aren't working too well at this hour. My mind is on the Lego board game we all played with Jacob last night. Right after our marvelous corned beef dinner, he cleared the coffee table of all the stuff we had brought with us.

Muffy had the complicated directions in her lap to help me. For the first hour, it appeared I might win. Jacob's expression faded as more and more of the pieces seemed to go my way.

But then, his fortune reversed, and he finally won as Trish pulled a pumpkin pie from the refrigerator. "I am the champion!" he said as he clenched his fists into the air. "I'm going to the Olympics!"

Then, he high-fived Gary and sat down to get pumpkin pie all over his face. I thought to myself how wonderful it is to be a 6-year-old boy in love with his family and in this place.

Excuse me, the coffee is ready, and so am I for a cup. Thank you for waiting.

Ahh, that's better. As you can tell, I'm writing this diary page in real time. I enjoy doing that sometimes. This Starbucks Breakfast Blend is the right stuff on a morning like this.

The sea is turning a light blue now as is the sky. There are white cloud puffs settling over the Maui hills that seem to be holding back the sea.

It's still too early for the sunbathers. Susan said yesterday that some women ought to realize they are not bikini kids anymore. Admitting the ravages of time is not easy. Certainly for me it isn't.

I can't remember exactly when it was I began combing my hair with a washcloth. It was probably when what hair I had left stopped being blond and began being white.

The sea now is turning to a deeper shade of blue. I wish you could hear it as it laps ashore and also the birds gathering along the guardrail. I watched Jacob talking to a dove the other morning, and Trish swears she heard the dove talking back.

We are going to hate leaving this place. Now, the doves are really serenading us. The sun is up! Trish still sleeps, though. The shadows are long and are keeping pace with the joggers I see puffing along below me.

My God, look at that heavenly rainbow arching just outside my window right this minute! The sea now is turning a deep blue. What a beautiful morning! What a great day to be alive!

The rainbow is gone, but it will always be Maui's gift to me. Trish is awake. She'll be sorry she missed the rainbow.

We leave tomorrow. Aloha.

March 13

Paradise present and paradise past

GINZA.

It's almost over, our Hawaiian vacation, that is. Trish, Muffy, Susan and I patrolled Front Street in Lahaina this morning and had an absolutely superb lunch at Kimo's.

I know it sounds crazy, but the old camp song, "Kimo, Ki Mo, Da Who Wah, Diddy High, Diddy Ho, Diddy Nip Sack, Rip Sack, Little Dog, Hokey Pokey, Sing Song, Kinna Kitch Ee Kigh Me, Oh" popped into my head, but I kept my mouth shut.

Good thing I did. I know it doesn't sound particularly appetizing, but my beef and cheddar sandwich on sourdough bread was the best I ever had. The au jus was perfect, and the fresh pineapple slice brought tears to my eyes.

The little Japanese-American lady who waited on Muffy and me when we bought her a nifty little black dress this morning seemed pleased when I spoke to her in the fractured Japanese I picked up more than 50 years ago in Tokyo.

Dick Becker, Bob Schutz, Nate Polowetzky, Bob Pierpoint and I sometimes prowled the Ginza during the war everyone has forgotten—the Korean War. We Lived at the Tokyo Correspondents' Club, next to the Russian Embassy where we regularly squirted Red Star guards with loaded seltzer bottles.

Those were the days. The little Japanese lady in Lahaina reminded me of them. She was so sad that she and her mother had never been able to visit Japan. I am also sad I was never able to return again to the beauty of Kamakura and its beautiful volcanic sand beaches and to the rocky shore at Itazuke where girls dived for pearls.

People tell me I would never recognize the Tokyo I knew then or South Korea's capital, Seoul. I left it when peace was supposed to be declared. There was only one paved road connecting North and South Korea then.

But the 2 nations seem separated by more now than they were then. I wonder how it will ever be possible to reunite them. Of course, I said the same thing in 1950 when I was ducking in and out of East and West Germany.

Now that the Germanys have been brought back together, their problems are by no means solved. It takes more than just redrawing maps to make it possible for their people to find a way to live together again.

And so here I sit at Muffy's laptop, trying to remedy age-old dilemmas. I have enjoyed the day, though, remembering old times, old friends and old problems that may never be solved.

We leave tomorrow night at 10, returning to Denver at 10 the next morning. I wonder if my tired old rear end can take it. I don't know where I would have been without Trish to help me this far.

March 14

Ugly fear robs old folks, kids of common bond

Dirty.

I could hear them giggling and laughing before I opened my eyes in the morning. It was such a pleasant sound. I love hearing children having fun anywhere.

These little kids were identical twin girls. They were chasing waves that were washing ashore on Kaanapali Beach. They had been building sand castles. There were 4 of them.

I have often wondered why kids always seem to build 4 sand castles, not 3, not 2, but 4. Anyhow, they were having a good time and I loved watching them.

A couple of hours later, they and their parents got on the elevator where Trish and I were. I leaned over, smiled at them and started to speak to them. But fear darkened their faces, and they turned away.

Their father, seeing I was with Trish and just a harmless old guy pulling an oxygen tank, tried to reassure them, but it was too late for me to try to make new friends.

I know what happened. Their father had probably told them over and over again not to talk to old men they didn't know. It was the right thing for him to do. I would have done the same thing had I been their father.

How rotten it is that we have let perverts build a wall between children and old people. As I have often written before, children and old folks need each other. They have many common interests.

When I see little ones in supermarkets where we shop, I am always tempted to speak to them, to tell them stories I know they would like to hear, to let them know I just want to be a friend.

It is embarrassing for all of us, though, when their mothers pull them away. They will warn their children that maybe I am probably nothing but a dirty old man who will hurt them.

The little ones are frightened. I want to run away and hide somewhere out of sight where there are no mothers, no children, no anyone to see what a fumbling old fool I have become.

This is all so wrong, isn't it?

When I ask myself this question, I look at our Jacob, and I understand how important it has become to protect our children. Was it always this way?

Is rampant pedophilia a modern phenomenon, or are media to blame for pouncing on each new case and blowing it out of proportion?

I sure don't know. I just know that I wish those 2 little girls had smiled back at me instead of turning away to their father with fear on their faces.

March 15

Maui? Wowie, what a place

DRAB.

Sorry, folks, but that's exactly how dear old Denver looked when our United airliner touched down at DIA after 10 days in lush, green Maui.

Oh, how I hated to leave it. I also hated to leave behind a Dove vanilla ice cream bar and a Haagen-Dazs dark-chocolate ice cream bar nestled beside it in the frozen-food compartment of the refrigerator in our condominium.

I am sure that Dolly, the smiling maid from Tonga who kept our condo spic and span, didn't leave them behind. I hope not.

I miss Maui right this minute. I missed it during the 10 hours we spent in the plane flying home. I shall always miss it. But I'll never see it again, and Maui will just have to remain stored away in my memories.

It's difficult, though, just to imagine trade winds that swayed palm trees outside my window, or the sound of the surf that pounded away at our sandy beach, or rainbows that emerged so quickly in the morning mists, or cloud banks that hovered over Maui's verdant hills, or so much more that elevated the spirit of this tired old man.

I am making such a fuss over Maui because I think that anyone who can possibly afford to make this journey should do so. I shall always be grateful I had the good fortune to make it possible for some members of my family.

Our little Jacob will never forget his boat ride to see the whales in Lahaina harbor. As they dived and spouted, they were so near to him that Trish had to grab him by the britches to keep him from falling into the Pacific.

He laughed and hollered and laughed and hollered some more as the great mammals emerged from the sea after diving under his boat. He wanted to touch them. It was an adventure Muffy, Susan, Gary and Trish will never forget, even though Trish had some queasy feelings.

As I wrote to a friend after returning from Maui—don't let time slip through your fingers and postpone the opportunity Gary had to scuba dive and swim with a school of dolphins as though he were one of them.

Look, you only come this way once, and you shouldn't cheat yourself of the opportunity of communing with the natural world around you in the beautiful Pacific.

Susan doesn't know how to scuba dive, but now she wants to learn. She did get to snorkel with tropical fish and see an underwater world she had only imagined before. Of course, I was on the sidelines for most of this.

You see, I had let time slip between my fingers and never had the experiences. Too old, now, dammit, but it was a thrill for me just to get to watch and share vicariously in their excitement.

Sure, I did a lot of what-might-have-been thinking over there. I thought of myself on a motorcycle again, bending that sucker around those narrow, winding roads. I thought of myself with styled hair, wearing styled jeans, hanging out in Maui's expensive hotels and making big talk in trendy Maui bars.

Hey, I can still dream big dreams, can't I?

I hope the adventure was as special for Muffy, Susan, Gary and Jacob as Trish and I hoped it would be. They all mean so much to us.

Aloha.

March 18

Pill helps 'old kid' focus during fast-fading days

FOCUSED.

What a nifty day this has been! I had no idea what was turning it around for me until Trish told me about this little half methylphenidate pill. It's prescribed for me twice each day before 1 p.m. Its short name is Ritalin.

It comes in 5mg tablets, so we have to cut the little sucker in half. That is almost impossible, so our hospice nurse gave us a little pill cutter. I have always hated it when we have to cut scored pills in half. The pills just crumble in your thumbnail. This razor-sharp little gizmo makes it a breeze.

I have been on fire all day. I cranked out a column in record time this morning. Did my wash and folded it. I have always done my own wash. Goes back to Army days, I guess. Doug Miller picked me up for a 5 p.m.

drink. It was a Coke. No beer so long as I am on morphine. Even a little alcohol with that stuff, and it's bad news.

I have mentioned Doug before. He's like a third son, and I wanted to hear all about Michelle and the kids. I can't believe Caitlin is ready for college. It was only yesterday that Doug was playing whiffle ball with my two sons, Brett and Jon, and Howie Bannock in the backyard where they wore a hole in my grass under the cottonwood.

I managed to slip into old jeans this afternoon instead of my daily uniform of faded sweats. Trish and I then went to dinner at Tops, where I did justice to a large slab of baby back ribs with coleslaw and fries. Sticky, sticky, sticky.

We hurried back home to catch *NYPD Blue*. I was still hungry, though, so I had a chocolate-covered vanilla ice cream Dove bar. I may have another before I go to bed if that box of Godiva dark chocolates Doug gave me doesn't kill my appetite.

Today, Trish picked up a couple of boxes of paper clips for me. I am trying to get my income tax records organized so if I die before April 15 I won't be leaving her a mess. I can't do it all myself, but if I can just somehow get my records organized for my tax guy, Doug Barr, we'll be miles ahead.

You know something? This world is just filled with nice people if you give them a chance. I know I am particularly fortunate because of who I am and what I do. People know me because of my column.

For example, who should call me on the telephone before our recent trip to Maui but Ralph Donahue. He is the optician who owned Western Optical, where I have been purchasing my glasses for more than 30 years.

Ralph said he had been following my columns about our trip, and thought maybe I might need some extra glasses. He is retired now, but was happy to come out to my house to fit me. How is that for being a nice guy?

I have known Ralph many years and have trusted him with my eyes for all that time.

I suppose that little Ritalin pill pepped me up. I know it is prescribed for children with attention-deficit disorder. Let me tell you something: This old kid is not having any trouble keeping focused these fast-disappearing days, or weeks, or months, or whatever time I have left. And I am grateful for that.

An avalanche of mail; a snowball of reply

DISTORTED.

My torrent of mail continues, and I wish there were a way I could acknowledge all of it, but I can't sit that long at the computer. I should mention that Carl Beverly Bledsoe dropped me a nice note in which he wrote that when he was in the legislature there were three reporters he trusted.

The other two were Carl Hilliard and Fred Brown. Bev writes that he "admires my fortitude in the face of death." He is also 78 and hopes he can emulate me.

Piece of cake, Bev. Everyone's gotta go. So can you.

Fred's name popped up in another letter I received from Bev, who writes he has found friends he can trust in Fred, John Sanko and Peter Blake, and two new *Rocky* staffers, Michele Ames and Peggy Lowe.

I treasure a wonderful letter from the Biography Channel's gifted Harry Smith. It is way too flattering to reprint here, except to report, "I dug out the sacred choral works of Vivaldi when I knew I was going to sit down and write this. I first heard 'Beatus Vir' on your show. It's Psalm 111, a psalm of thanksgiving."

That's so nice, Harry, and I hope you're reading this way back in New York City, where you and Joyce are raising your family.

I'm delighted Harry mentioned Vivaldi's choral works, which I adore, too. When I say Vivaldi wrote 400 concerti, his critics will always say he wrote the same concerto 400 times. Bushwa!

I am pleased so many folks responded to the interview I gave to National Public Radio and how many of them enjoyed the Friday Waltz. Thanks should really go to my friend, Don Kinney, who video-taped one of my regular Friday Waltzes for reasons I never understood. Maybe he did it just for the fun of it.

Anyhow, an audiotape was dubbed from it for use on NPR. I really had to laugh, though, when I received a distorted voice-mail message from Binghamton, N.Y., thanking me for my Tuesday Waltz that was just played on the radio.

The only person I know who lives in Binghamton is Amy Shapiro, who once showed up to dance my Friday Waltz in person, in a green taffeta ball gown.

She had to have been behind the Binghamton broadcast. Once something is broadcast over the radio, it isn't a secret anymore.

Did I ever acknowledge the gift Bill Gallo sent me? He calls it "Concerto for Geno," and he and his son have dubbed on CD some of their favorite jazz pieces they know I shall enjoy. Indeed I do, and so do friends who have borrowed it from me.

Bill, in case you didn't know, is the best newspaper writer I know working anywhere. You can read his movie reviews and columns in *Westword*. I used to sit next to him at the *Rocky*. I just wish some of that talent had rubbed off on me.

I cherish all those 25 years I worked in the *Rocky Mountain News* newsroom. I miss all that energy now that I am working alone at home. I learned so much from those with whom I worked downtown, and I had so much fun there, too.

When I hear young reporters grouse about their work and how they are treated, I remind them these are the good old days. Some day, they will understand that.

March 20

Hospice is about 'comfort care'

LOST WEEKEND.

No, I didn't booze my way through Sunday. I stopped abusing myself that way many years ago. My body temperature had soared to 102. Even so, I had terrible chills and a lot of pain. I don't recall being conscious for much of this.

There didn't seem to be any reason for these symptoms, so Trish conferred with my doctor and my hospice nurse, and it was decided to admit me to City Park Care Center for 24-hour observation. It is one of Hospice of Metro Denver's residence care centers. It is located in the old Presbyterian/St. Luke's Hospital.

When I regained consciousness Monday morning, I didn't know where I was or what had happened to me. My family was all there: Susan, Jon, Brett, Muffy and, of course, Trish.

And so I am out of the care center and home now and feel better now that Trish has explained what happened to me. As I have written before, I am indeed fortunate to have a caregiver as talented as she.

Trish is a registered nurse and worked for nine years as volunteer coordinator for Exempla hospice care at Lutheran Medical Center. I keep wondering how tough it is for people who are dying and who don't have the quality support I have.

One of the things I hope my diary will accomplish is to urge families of dying patients to have their physicians refer them to one of the many hospice organizations in this area. There is so much misunderstanding about hospice.

It is a whole philosophy of giving dying patients what hospice calls "comfort care." Many patients, like me, prefer to die at home. This is possible if there is a good caregiver at home.

It doesn't have to be someone with professional training, like Trish. It can be a wife or husband who can be trained or educated in the caring of a dying loved one. When the end of life is near and the demands are too great for the caregiver, the patient can be moved to a residence facility for life's end.

I have explained this before, but somehow the message doesn't always get through. I have spoken to physicians about hospice. They don't always understand it.

Anyhow, I'm glad to be home again, and I enjoyed the ride here tremendously. As we traveled south on York Street, Trish noticed I was craning my neck as we passed East Eighth Avenue. "Are you doing a little life reflection?" she asked.

Of course, I was. I remembered the floral paintings I cherished on the ceilings of 740 York St. before we moved to 2315 E. Seventh Ave. Parkway. What a big old house that was! I bought it from Louis Mack. He sold it to me when he became too old to take care of it. I lost it when my first marriage went down the tubes.

There were happy memories on the drive home, though. We passed our old neighborhood near 12th and Vine where Trish and I lived when we married. We often ducked into the IHOP on East Colfax Sunday morning for waffles smothered with whipped cream and fresh strawberries. I miss that.

I showered and shaved when we finally arrived home. I didn't like what I saw in the mirror as I stood there, buck naked. My weight is down to 126, and my spine is twisted to the left. I can't stand up straight anymore. This dying is ugly business.

This is one of those days when I wish I could get it over with, if you don't mind my ending an awkward sentence with a preposition. Still, though, I am happy to be home and want to talk to my kids on the telephone.

March 26

Barrett's Homer inspired Poitier

Bridges.

How nice it was to watch Sidney Poitier acknowledge the praise given him Monday night at the Academy Awards ceremony. As he smiled in appreciation, his face also appeared before me as it had years ago in a Denver hotel room where I interviewed him.

It was just a few months after he had been the first African-American to be honored by the Academy for his best-actor performance. He enjoyed recounting to me the pleasure he had received that night.

As he did, he spoke admiringly of William E. Barrett, the author who created the role of Homer Smith in his book, *The Lilies of the Field.* It was that portrayal of an itinerant handyman that won Poitier the Academy Award.

By today's standards, the film probably would not have been considered extraordinary or worthy of Academy Award recognition. It was black and white and had no big-name stars to hype its box office appeal. But it had Poitier, whose honest charm played out so appealingly against a cloister of make-believe nuns.

Because Bill Barrett had been a close friend of mine for many years, I was eager to talk to him about his reaction to the casting of Poitier as Homer Smith. "I couldn't have been happier at the choice," he said those many years ago.

Then he leaned back in his chair at his old Pennsylvania Street apartment across from the Governor's Mansion. He cradled his Scotch on the rocks in his hands, and spoke of the night Poitier received the Academy Award. "Almost the minute the ceremony had ended, he went to a telephone to call and thank me for creating Homer, a character almost tailor-made for him."

Barrett has been dead for years now, but his many novels still remind us of the literary gifts he bestowed, not only on Sidney Poitier, but on all of us. Some of them include *The Empty Shrine, The Sudden Strangers, The Shadows of the Images, Woman on Horseback, Flight from Youth* and *The Left Hand of God*, which was made into a motion picture starring Humphrey Bogart as an escaped convict dressed as a priest.

Bill showed me a letter from Bogart in which he apologized for not playing a priest with more conviction. "All they would let me do," Bogart wrote, "was pat a little kid on the head." Almost all of Bill's books were written around a Roman Catholic theme.

When I asked about that, Bill said, "I grew up as a Catholic. Its teachings were close to me. I think any writer uses his life experiences in his writing. I wasn't preaching to anyone. I was just writing what I knew best."

There were other novels, including *The Edge of Things*, in which he wrote an inscription to me about our mutual respect for the craft of writing. "Good writing is a bridge on which minds meet, a bridge that the writer must build."

How true that is. Barrett's portrayal of Homer Smith did not involve a bridge constructed of big words, or long literary-style sentences, or cumbersome paragraphs. It was the simplicity of Barrett's writing that brought Homer Smith to life and helped Poitier give us a performance of a lifetime.

Bill was the father of the late Marge Barrett, who spent most of her adult life as a feature writer for the *Rocky Mountain News*. I still cherish my many conversations with Bill about the skill of bridge-building in writing and how he began writing World War I aviation dime novels for only a penny a word.

March 29

Easter eggs bring back basketful of memories

TWIRLY TOPS.

Here it is a few days before Easter, and I am wondering if there are still any hidden Easter eggs on South Depew Street. We lived next door to the Haggerty family there for 30 years.

Never an Easter Sunday passed but what friends and families of the Haggertys, and their kids, fanned out across back yards in search of Paas-dyed Easter eggs. I can close my eyes and still see Chipper and

Kelly, baskets in hands, looking under every shrub, every bush, every drain spout.

Of course they never found them all. Sometimes we would spot them later on in the summer, or even the next fall. Watching Patrick scurrying around hiding the eggs made my day. He and his wife, Jan, are gone now, but I still have precious memories of them on Easter Sunday.

Patrick never lost his sense of humor. As he lay dying at Swedish Hospital, his twin sister, a Roman Catholic nun, told him a priest was there to give him last rites. He was barely able to open his eyes and managed a little smile as he asked, "Do I have to tip this guy?"

Somehow, we have all managed to preserve the ritual of dyeing Easter eggs for our little ones. At first, we pretended the Easter Bunny brought them the baskets filled with eggs, and then we let them in on the secret and they helped us dye the eggs.

Not much has changed in the Paas Easter Egg Coloring Kit over the years. There are still the six cold water fizz coloring tablets, the copper wire egg dipper, the four egg holders. In recent years, Paas has added nine twirly tops, 29 Easter stickers and one punch-out animal hunt puzzle.

I noticed on the Paas box that it now has a Web site. I tried logging onto it, but all I found was a big picture of colored Easter eggs. There could have been more information, but I am probably too clumsy with computers to find it.

For me, Easter fun always came when little kids are old enough to make up Easter baskets for other children. They would fill them with eggs, candy and little toys and leave them on the doorsteps of other children. Then they would ring the doorbell and scoot away, pretending they were the Easter Bunny.

I remember one Easter Trish and I did that. It is wonderful fun for adults, too. I don't think there is anyone who gets a bigger kick out of Easter than Trish. She starts thinking about it weeks in advance.

Of course, this Easter, probably my last, will be very special because of Jacob, our 6-year-old grandson. He talks of little else these days and spends much of his time looking out the front window of his home in hope of Easter surprises.

Experience has indicated to me that little girls are better at egg dyeing than little boys. The boys are impatient and want to remove the eggs from the dye too soon. I can remember egg-dyeing sessions when I was a little kid and we lived next door to the Walton family.

Betty Lee was probably about a year older than I, and she was always so much better at dyeing eggs. She would leave them in the dye for the allotted three minutes. They came out bright and beautiful. Mine were sort of a limpy pastel because I wanted to take them out too soon.

Isn't it amazing what Easter memories will stay with you for more than 30, even 70 years?

April 1

The Haggerty heritage: a twinkle worth repeating

IMAGINATION.

Before you sit down to dash off an e-mail complaining about my Pat Haggerty story I wrote in my column last week, there is an explanation. Yes, I have written the story before, maybe even twice.

Your first thought may be "memory loss," an affliction we older scouts suffer all the time. There are days when the names of my progeny sometimes escape me for a few moments.

I suppose I could mount the Andy Rooney defense. As I recall it, he became angry that his readers failed to understand the demands of cranking out this kind of stuff all the time and occasional repetition ought to be overlooked.

None of the above. I repeated the story of how Pat, on his death bed, asked his twin sister, Patricia, if he had to tip the priest who came to give him the last rites. It's a wonderful story and says much about the twinkle always present in his personality.

I first heard it at his funeral from his sister, a Roman Catholic nun who spoke so eloquently about him at the ceremony. Was his funeral a ceremony? I am not sure what to call it. It was a gathering of his friends and the family who survived him. We all laughed when she told it. She has a twinkle, too, as does his other sister, Alice.

It is wonderful for us that the twinkle has been inherited by those who are part of the Haggerty heritage. Haggerty heritage! That has a nice ring to it.

So, anyhow, those of us in the column writing game reach out to grab whatever we can to make our points. Speaking of that, Patrick was some kind of man. He was a premier National Football League referee for the more than 30 years that I knew him.

He was a Northside kid who played professional baseball before he became an NFL referee. He just didn't know how to quit. Quit wasn't in him.

For the last 2 years of his life, I watched him run up and down the football field, suffering the agony of prostate cancer. He had pain big time, but he twinkled right through it, game after game after game. No one knew but his family and close friends.

I could tell he was suffering the last year of his life, but I never heard him complain, even once. He tried every kind of treatment there was. He traveled to both coasts for help, but nothing worked. Patrick never complained. He just kept twinkling, always smiling through his pain.

Every year when football fanatics complain about referees and how they ought to work full time as do players and not hold jobs in business and industry as they do now, I think that is a lot of bushwah.

I wonder what they would do between weekends. Would they go out to Invesco Field at Mile High (arragh, pardon me while I gag on that)? Would they go out there and throw flags at imaginary players running imaginary plays?

Would they blow whistles at each other and look at challenged plays on video screens? Would they look at films of imaginary games? Just what would they do Monday through Friday?

Well, that's my Patrick Haggerty column for today. I may write about his last rites again, that is if I need to, to make a point.

April 2

Easter morning: syrup, serendipity

SERENDIPITY.

"What a day this has been, what a rare mood I'm in ..." Well it wasn't exactly like being in love. But it was one of the most wonderful Easter mornings in my memory. Perfect. Absolutely perfect.

It began when Trish awakened me to a superb French toast breakfast. She adores making French toast, maybe because she adores eating French toast.

Her batter consisted of fresh eggs, of course, whisked with a splash of milk, a dash of cinnamon, a squirt of vanilla extract and a tablespoon of Harvey's Bristol Cream Sherry.

Then—this is important—the bread she uses is inch-thick slices of Udi's Challah Classic Breaded Egg Bread made with flour, water, eggs, butter, sugar, salt, milk, sea salt and cornmeal.

After she splashes the slices into the batter and slips them onto the oiled skillet, she browns each one evenly on both sides and serves them slathered with Kerrygold Pure Irish Butter.

Frankly, I have never been a fan of fancy syrups. Good old Log Cabin is good enough for me. While I pigged out on French toast, Trish began to hide Easter eggs for Jacob in the back yard. I'm too crippled up for that anyhow.

By then, it was time for us to assemble the Easter dinner for our family. We had been working on it for days. You never know how many Easters you have left.

I did take time out to try to call Dorothy Fuller Smith in Tasmania. Our friendship goes back to 1945 when World War II ended and the two of us shared the excitement of V-E Day in London.

I wanted to talk to her about the death of the Queen Mum whom we both had seen that long ago night. I couldn't get through, though. Damn these phone companies and their electronic menus.

By then, our family began arriving for dinner. Trish had decided on a spiral-cut ham from Costco, which turned out to be a masterpiece. She glazed it with light corn syrup, curry powder and grated orange peel.

Jacob was scurrying around the yard looking for Easter eggs. The squirrels had found some of them first, though, and probably got a little sick on chocolate bunnies.

Susan brought her award-winning scalloped potatoes. Muffy brought fruit salad with mangoes in it, and, oh yes, days before, I whipped up my famous Capt. Sunshine's baked beans in our old cast-iron pot.

I soaked Great Northern white beans overnight, and simmered them in the morning until they started to pop in a kettle, added a cup of brown sugar and another cup of Brer' Rabbit molasses.

Then, I whacked up 2 pounds of salt pork and 2 large onions and simmered them in the cast-iron pot. I added the bean mixture and covered the pot and slow baked it in the oven at about 250 degrees for a bunch of hours until I liked the way the beans tasted.

When we sat down to eat, the sun was shining through the window and Trish fashioned several decorative towels into a curtain to keep it from Jacob's eyes.

The towels were sent to us years ago by Dorothy, whose daughter-in-law, Loretta Vonthien-Smith, had hand-painted them and blocked them on linen in Tasmania.

I wish you could see them.

They are red-flowering gum Eucalyptus ficifolia, leatherwood Eucryphia lucida, and deciduous beech Nothofagus gunnii.

Of course, you knew who was calling when the phone rang. It was Dorothy. Are we talking serendipity here, or what?

April 3
When I'm awake, I'm appreciative

EMBARRASSMENT.

I spent much of Easter weekend working my way through another big box of e-mail and snail-mail messages from readers concerned about my health. They help me focus where I am in my dying and death process.

There are mornings when I find it so difficult to wake up and get out of bed. My spine is becoming more twisted to the left, leaving my ribs resting on my hip. This is quite painful, and I am grateful for the relief prescribed by my hospice team.

Still, the best relief comes from sleep. At the beginning of this process, my hospice nurse told me I would sleep a great deal as death approached. I don't feel, though, that death is near. Honestly, I wish it would come sooner than later.

My family has been absolutely wonderful with my care. Sometimes, I just don't understand how Trish puts up with me and my needs. She is so patient and kind. I don't see my sons and daughters every day, but they call me on the telephone. My 6-year-old grandson, Jacob, is an absolute delight in what is left of my life. I am so sorry I shall not live long enough to see him develop into manhood as my grandfather did in my life.

Jacob adores his aunts and uncles, particularly Jon, with whom he has a special relationship. The other day, he and Jon were sitting in Jon's 1968 Firebird that Jon has owned and cherished for 27 years. He and I restored it again and again.

Anyhow, Jacob is sitting behind the steering wheel, pretending he is driving by turning the wheel and shifting the gear lever. Jon said to him, "Someday, Jacob, I want this car to be yours. I am saving it for you until you grow up."

Jacob continues steering the wheel in his drive to wherever his imagination is taking him. He glances casually out the side window and says a single word, "Cool." Is that some kind of kid, or what?

Now, about those messages. I deeply appreciate all the prayers being said on my behalf. I know they are sincere, and I am sincerely grateful for them. Even though I may not share the denominational beliefs of some readers, it doesn't mean I am unappreciative.

Most readers respect my need for privacy. The hospice chaplain checks on me regularly, but he is not intrusive and doesn't seek to impose any kind of faith on me at this critical point in my life.

Similarly, there is a pastor living a few doors from me here in Lakewood who stops by occasionally to chat—mostly about anything I wish to talk about, not necessarily his beliefs.

Just up on the hill, near where I live, is the Loretto Center, where a number of nuns of the Sisters of Loretto live. I have known and respected them since the center was built many years ago. My beloved Sister Mary Louise Beutner, "Lamb Chop" as I called her, squired me through the center when it was still a novitiate, causing young novices to scream and whoop with embarrassment that a man was there.

The center is now a residence for retired sisters. The building is also used as a school for children with special-education needs. The nuns still living there have let me know they, too, are praying for me. How I love and respect them all!

On the other hand, I resent those who want to convert me, or even frighten me. They, no doubt, are answering their perception of an evangelical requirement of their faith. I hope they are not offended by my rejection of their attempts. Their prayers are welcome, though, as are those from others who are concerned about my well-being.

April 5

Eddie's passing sailed right past me

Leggy.

I hate funerals, but had I been able to walk, I would have attended the funeral March 1 at Whatley Chapel at the University of Denver Law School Campus for former Colorado Supreme Court Chief Justice Edward Pringle. Eddie, as his close friends called him, would hate that sentence.

"Too long," he would have said scornfully. "I shouldn't have to tell that to you newspaper guys." My old pal, Suzanne Weiss, reminded me he once was in line for a sports reporter job at *The Denver Post*.

Instead, he attended law school. After graduating from North High School at age 16, he studied at the University of Colorado, graduating with a law degree when he was just 22, wrote Nick Groke in the *Post*.

News of his death slipped by me. Was I looking the other way? Why didn't some of his old reporters-turned-lawyers call me? This kind of thing seems to happen all the time. We newspaper guys aren't paying attention when really important folks such as Eddie slip from the scene and deserve to be remembered.

Eddie had been ill for some time. After he retired as chief justice, the Colorado Bar Association wanted to honor him at its annual convention at the Broadmoor Hotel in Colorado Springs.

He would have none of it, though. Eddie didn't like honors. His mission later in life was to get lawyers to write their briefs in language everyday folks could understand. He was fed up with legalistic gobbledygook designed to keep you and me from finding out the truth.

The bar association wanted to honor him for that crusade, but Eddie just wanted to stay home. For reasons I never understood, he was a fan of mine. He loved my nostalgia pieces in the *Rocky*. I despise making speeches, but I made an exception that time because of my admiration for a guy most folks rate as one of Colorado's best Supreme Court justices.

And so the bar association came up with a strategy to lure him to the Broadmoor. They enlisted my help through another reporter-turned-lawyer, a young woman who had done stand-ups at Channel 7 before law school, and who was also a friend of mine. She persuaded me to help convince Eddie. And if you admire leggy brunettes, you can understand why the strategy worked.

Anyhow, Eddie showed up to get his plaque, and I talked for 20 minutes about the fun we all had in north Denver when we were young and full of you-know-what and vinegar, and we all went home happy.

I really liked the lawyers with whom Eddie practiced before Gov. Steve McNichols tapped him for the high court. He worked elbow to elbow with former Attorney General Duke Dunbar and fiery defense lawyer Max Melville, who was also a crack prosecutor.

He also worked with former Chief Justice Fred Winner, a pal of my former boss, *Rocky* Editor Michael Balfe Howard. Don't you love all these names? We can't let ourselves forget them.

Certainly, we can't forget another reporter-turned-lawyer, Edward Day, who also ascended to the high court.

Eddie Pringle was one of a kind. He was a teacher, lawyer and World War II veteran whose stained-glass portrait is in the Colorado Supreme Court window. Eddie, I am sorry I am so late in recognizing what you have done for your beloved state of Colorado.

April 6
Blues may come, but Paris never lets go

FILTHY.

Boy, do I ever have the blues today. These 4 walls are really closing in on me. I think our trip to Hawaii spoiled me. I'm fed up with writing about death and dying. What the heck is left to say, anyhow?

What can I do? I have cleaned my hearing aids and put a new battery in my desk clock. I popped another Inderol pill to keep my hands from shaking. I opened a new pack of Big Red gum and a new bottle of Dasani to keep my whistle wet.

I had a chat with the oxygen delivery guy about the weather. I made out a check to Trish for the groceries. That has been my day.

It was nice to see Jon when he stopped by to pick up some X-rays this afternoon to take to my doctor. We decided the Rockies are going to stink up the season in much the same way the Nuggets and the Broncos rendered the same kind of odor to their seasons. Boring.

There is more to my blues than just my closed-in environment. My planned trip to Paris is off. I know, I wrote that when I returned from Hawaii, I wanted to go to Paris and write about what I saw and what I felt.

My hospice nurse told me it was just too "risky." Some of my family members feel the same way, and I am sure my doctor would agree. Traveling in the United States is one thing, but traveling in a foreign country with my disabilities would be much more challenging.

I don't think people understand why I want to return to Paris. "You've been there and done that," they seem to be saying, as though Paris is just another Disneyland. "Once you have seen the Magic Kingdom, why do you want to see it again?" they are sort of asking.

That's difficult to explain. You see, Paris never lets go of you. It becomes a part of you always. Sure, I have seen the Eiffel Tower and don't need to see it again. That's not the point. It's feeling Paris again and being there again.

The war did it to me. When it ended, I went "over the hill" with a crazy Polish-American priest and a cavalry farm boy who wanted to see the "City of Lights" as much as I did.

It was tossing a few at Pig Alley (Place Pigalle) and marching around Mere Catherine's bistro on Montmartre with a bunch of ancient French soldiers in old uniforms that didn't fit anymore. It was sleeping under the bridge at Pont Neuf in our filthy bedrolls.

It was dodging "snowdrop" MPs who were trying to round up us vagrant warriors before we had to return to our beloved Sixth Armored Division, which probably hadn't missed us yet, anyhow. It was that kind of thing.

I wanted to feel all that again in beautiful Paris. Do you blame me? Ce vas! Or something like that.

I know that doesn't mean much to folks who weren't there and didn't feel the giddiness that the big war was over, and you were going home to friends, family and your job. How could you understand that if you weren't there?

So that's why I have the blues today. I'll get over it. I'll just go to Paris in my dreams, in my memories. Those things will all be there.

Succumbing again to the allure of fine poetry

Coppers.

When Thomas Hornsby Ferril died, I thought I would never be interested in poetry again. He was more than Colorado's poet laureate. He was my friend. We drank together, laughed together, even sang together.

I collected all of his books about poetry and those that were not. His death was a deep personal loss to me. On Good Friday every year, I read aloud over my radio station what I considered his masterpiece, "The Prairie Melts."

The first year after I began work here at the *Rocky Mountain News*, I convinced our editor, Michael Balfe Howard, that we should reprint it again on Good Friday, 1979. Michael left the *Rocky*, and the tradition ended.

Still, I always read it to myself on Good Friday as I did this year. It's on Page 14 of his *New and Selected Poems*, published in 1952. Over a small prairie flower he had drawn inside, Tom autographed the book, "To Gene Amole one morning when the prairie was melting back of Ruby Hill." The first line always catches in my throat:

> The prairie melts into the throats of larks
> And green like water begins to flow
> Into the pinto patches of the snow.

I have read the poem several times publicly, and each time, that first line conjures in my mind the vastness and the beauty of our prairie when spring is here.

How I love this poem and love it more now that I read, an old man tapping the world in springtime with a stick. I guess I am taking the poem more personally than before.

My interest in poetry has been reawakened with books by Thomas Lynch, *Still Life in Milford* and *Bodies in Motion and At Rest*. I wrote recently about his wonderful *The Undertaking: Life Studies from the Dismal Trade.*

He was kind enough to send me his first two volumes of poetry and essays from his home in Milford, Mich., where he is a funeral director and writes about life and death. From *Still Life in Milford*, let me give a sample from "The Moveen Notebook, In Memory of Nora Lynch":

> Tommy died in March of seventy one.
> I can still see him laid out in his bed
> a rosary laced among his fingers, thumbs
> curled the purple shroud, bright coppers on his eyelids,
> the Missal propped between his chest and chin
> as if to keep your man from giving out
> with whatever the dead know and the living don't …

Lynch writes about life and death in County Clare on the banks of the River Shannon. Somehow I wonder if he ever met Breda McGurk, as I had 52 years ago on a train from Limerick to Dublin along the River Shannon.

How would he have written about her copper hair, the sprinkle of freckles on her upturned nose and her pale blue eyes?

Would she have smiled at him and called him "Yank"?

Just wondering.

April 9

Death still at bay, so scrape my teeth

ROOTS.

No, this isn't about a search for the Amole family tree. It's about how I am living longer than I thought I would. You may recall that I canceled my appointment with dental hygienist Patty Hull when I thought I was going to die right away.

Who wants to get his roots scraped if he is about to go to the great newsroom in the sky? As much as I admired Patty and her devotion to painless care, I figured I would just skip the scraping in the belief that who needs periodontal care in the hereafter?

But here I am months later, still alive and kicking while the plaque is building up on my roots, and so I had better phone for an appointment to see Patty again. I actually had an appointment but had to break it when I had a lost weekend several weeks ago.

I had to return to the Hospice of Metro Denver Residence Care Center at the old Presbyterian/St. Luke's Hospital. I had lost consciousness, had fluid in my lungs and a temperature that broke 100. I am OK now, though, and am back on course.

So I must go back to see Patty again. In anticipation of my return, my friends at Cody Dental Clinic had prepared the most amazing welcome-back card I have ever seen. Trish brought it home to me Friday after what she believes to be her final visit to Cody for dental reconstruction.

I think that's what you could call it. It all began shortly after we were married. She fell on our front porch on South Depew Street, breaking off one of her front teeth. That's when her dental saga began.

First came a temporary tooth, which of course didn't match the other teeth. Next, it became apparent to Trish, that her teeth had been crooked since childhood and braces were not fitted then as they should have been.

OK, so then began the long process of being fitted with adult braces. This was about 30 years ago when folks were just beginning to become aware of the potential of adult orthodontics and cosmetic dentistry.

And so, Friday was a big day for Trish. No more retainers. No more braces, just the bright, beautiful smile she always wanted. And so she brought home this wonderful card to me, signed by all the Cody dentists, office workers and hygienists.

I wish you could see it. I have written earlier about how the late Dr. William Hiatt had successfully treated me for bloated gums and infected roots. I also mentioned how he and I resembled each other. Same color hair. Same kind of glasses. Same slender build, even though he was much more athletically inclined than I. Same prominent nose. (That's putting it kindly.)

Receptionist Lori Boomer wrote about it in the card, recalling the time I was waiting in the lobby when a patient came in, sat down beside me and began to complain about her symptoms.

Lordy, I had forgotten that and couldn't stop laughing when I read Lori's description of my dilemma that day when I kept trying to interrupt her to tell her I wasn't Dr. Hiatt and was just waiting to get my roots scraped.

Anyhow, I am still alive and somewhat kicking and will get one of my sons to take me in to Cody for my appointment with Patty and to thank them all for their kindness.

Here's my lowdown on glazed doughnuts

HORSEPLAY.

If you have been wondering what I do with all my spare time, I have been doing a thoughtful study of glazed doughnuts. I say "thoughtful" and not "scientific" because I still haven't worked my way through all the glazed doughnuts available.

When I brought a selection of Winchell's doughnuts to my pals at the old KVOD each morning, I would sneak out the only glazed doughnut in the box before the others came to work. I still find it necessary to differentiate between the old and the new KVODs because there is so much difference separating the two.

For example, old KVOD people seemed to have more fun than the new KVOD folk who deign on-the-air horseplay and occasional giggling. They are all so damned professional with their seamless, round-the-clock fund raising. But, it is their ballgame, and I should be grateful that they rescued classical music from oblivion.

But back to doughnuts. I am not sure what the proper term for my daughter's father-in-law should be. His name is Tom Waters. Technically, I suppose, he is a father-in-law once-removed. Something like that, but that seems needlessly awkward. I finally settled on just calling him, "Friend Tom."

Anyhow, it was Friend Tom who introduced me to Krispy Kreme Donuts, and I have to say, they are the standard of the industry. I'm not sure I would wait in line for hours to buy them, but it was Friend Tom who did the waiting and the buying, and I was the guy who did the eating.

My friend, Doug Miller, brought me a box of LaMar's glazed doughnuts, supposedly superior to Krispy Kremes. They were close, but we aren't playing horseshoes here, and the Krispy Kremes are a shade better. LaMar's are six bucks a box and well worth it.

Trish often brings home an assortment of doughnuts from the Winchell's Donut House on South Wadsworth near where we live. This is nice because they are seductively warm when I open the box. Naturally, I go for the glazed doughnuts first, then maybe a Bismarck or one of those custard-filled buns they do so well.

I mustn't forget the apple fritter she brings for herself. Everytime I see an apple fritter I think of Steve Caulk, one of our ace business news writers who sat next to me when I still worked in the *Rocky* newsroom. Steve was hooked on apple fritters until he invoked his superior willpower and quit them cold turkey, he said.

It's risky to send out Trish for food. Last night she stopped by a little Japanese eatery in our neighborhood and came back with 50 bucks worth of sushi. I hadn't eaten sushi in more than 50 years when I was in the Far East pretending to be a correspondent covering the Korean War.

Anyhow, I had forgotten how I enjoyed the little raw nibbles and pigged out on them until they were gone.

But wait a minute! This column about food would not be complete without mentioning the sheer pleasure I received when I ate incredibly delicious Italian pizzelle cookies from Dorothy Pastore, a lovely north Denver Italian lady.

She baked me the most mouthwatering, anise pizzelles in my memory and sent her son out to deliver them to me late Saturday night. When I say mouthwatering, I mean just that! They are so delicate they actually melted on my tongue.

Thank you, Dorothy. I don't deserve these pizzelles, but I am going to eat them, every one.

April 11

Tom Gavin was right: God always provides

ALL TOGETHER.

When I was new at the column-writing game, I was stewing about what I would write the next day. T. Milliken Gavin told me not to worry. He cupped his hands together, holding them heavenward. "Do this," he said, "and God will provide."

In the years that have followed, I have followed his advice. God has always provided, not always with material of which I could be proud, but enough to get me through the day.

Such was the case Monday when my good neighbor and friend, Audrey Dummer, brought a letter to my house that had been misaddressed to her home.

She didn't realize it, but she was doing God's work this day by supplying me material for another page in my diary. It is just as well the letter was tightly sealed, because there were photographs in it showing me and others in Full Monty. That is to say we were all buck naked.

The letter was from Ross Folkard Mark, an Australian journalist with whom I had the good fortune to work covering the Korean War, or whatever the historians decided to call it, back in 1951. First off, I had no idea Ross had such a dramatic middle name.

The photographs, as Ross explained, were taken of the Imjin River Bathing and Chowder Society, of which I apparently was a member, as were Ross, Jim Becker and Bob Schutz of the Associated Press and a young soldier from the 7th Cavalry Regiment, once commanded by General George Armstrong Custer. How is that for detail you didn't need to know?

There was only one bar of soap between us. Some years back, Schutz came through Denver and assured me the photograph had been destroyed. Not so. It has survived, and it seems to me I wrote a column about this little pond from the Imjin River that served us so well as a place to bathe.

It was within easy walking distance of the 7th headquarters where we all billeted. One day, though, curiosity got the better of Becker, Schutz and me, and we decided to follow the Imjin upstream to see the source of the water in which we were bathing and frolicking daily.

We carefully reconnoitered our way along the stream for maybe 50 yards or so, finally stopping at what appeared to be something in the stream that diverted its flow. There were two Chinese soldiers, lying face-down in the water. They were very dead and very much in a state of decomposition.

So ended our bathing and frolicking in the Imjin River Bathing and Chowder Society. There is a splendid profile photograph of Ross displaying his charms. In thinking back on our adventure, I can recall Ross regaling us with stories of how swimming in the buff was nothing new to him, as youthful Australian men and women explored rivers this way all the time.

There are two photographs of me, one in which I am fully clothed and drinking a can of PX beer and the other lathering myself with Becker's bar of soap. Schutz is seated in the foreground, strategically screening out my Full Monty charms.

As Tom Gavin said, "God will provide." And as I added, it isn't always with material of which we all can be proud, but it is sufficient to get me through this day.

We can all be grateful that my diary is not illustrated with photographs.

April 12

My dad could even sell a dog a name

HORACE.

Let me tell you what the three most hated words in marketing are today. They are, "Some assembly required." I thought of them last night watching TV when one of those home improvement stores promised customers it would assemble power lawn mowers or outdoor barbecues at no extra charge. Wow!

I know stores are doing this because business is lousy. It's a great come-on because customers hate to buy something and find it will come to them in a box. I hate that.

When I see an advertisement with a picture of something I want to buy, I want it to look like that.

If I buy a lawn mower, I want it to look like a lawn mower. I don't want to have to go to the back of the store to pick up a heavy box on which are printed the hated words, "Some assembly required."

And so I think it is a clever marketing strategy that the store promises customers that no assembly is required. I am aware of these things because salesmanship is in my bones. My parents were outstanding sales people, as was I.

So was I. Anyone who ever heard me advertise Vollmer's apricot macaroon tortes on my old KVOD radio station will tell you that. Folks would just drool all over the place before I was through describing the tortes.

I tried passing along these marketing skills to my kids. It was always a pleasure observing my son, Jon, at work. I stood aside one night watching him work a guy who came into the store to buy a lawn mower.

He wasn't interested in one of those expensive power jobs, just something he could push. In no time at all, though, my son stepped up the guy higher and higher and HIGHER until he had sold him a lawn tractor.

It wasn't one of those el-cheapo jobs, either. It was a big, REALLY big, expensive lawn tractor with all the bells and whistles. And when I heard Jon say, "Let me put that together for you, sir," I couldn't have been more proud.

Did I mention that my father, Frank, was a crackerjack salesman? He was the absolute best. He could actually sell animals. I don't mean he could just sell animals to people as pets. He could sell animals on themselves, make them actually believe in themselves.

Many years ago when we lived in a little house on South Emerson Street, Pop admired a little dog that lived in our neighborhood. It wasn't one of those nervous pedigreed dogs, but just an ordinary, friendly little pup. The dog's name was "Brownie," or some other name Pop didn't think suited him.

And so he decided to change the dog's name to "Horace." It wasn't long until the dog refused to respond to the name Brownie, but only to Horace. The dog's owners didn't like it much, but Horace did, and that was the way it stayed.

When Pop whistled and called for Horace, the little dog's tail wagged and he actually seemed to smile as he trotted up to Pop and placed his cold nose against Pop's hand. That's salesmanship, old friend, real salesmanship.

April 13
Several bright lights from my past go dark

ELEGANCE.

This is being written on Thursday. Folks ask me how I stay busy. My phone rang early this morning with a call from Stan Thies, a *Denver Post* reporter I knew 40 years ago. He told me Lee Olson had died.

I hated hearing that. Lee was such a kind, gentle soul. He worked for Bill Hosokawa on the *Post's* editorial page, and after retirement wrote several Western history books. The most recent was about England's "remittance men," rich, young ne'er-do-wells whose fathers sent them over to the new world to earn their keep.

Then I picked up the *Rocky* to read that my old friend, Leondele "Moose" LaMiaux had died in Bozeman, Mont. He was 74. I hated reading that, too. Moose and I worked together during the early years after WGN of Chicago had purchased Channel 2 with the promise it would make it competitive with Channels 4, 7 and 9.

I was signed on as the news anchorman, and Moose often directed our newscasts. Our relationship was rocky at first. When the script called for us to go to film, or to tape, or to a still picture, the shot wouldn't be ready and the camera lingered on me.

There I sat, with nothing to do or say. After the show, I would rage at him, "Moose, Moose, you left me with egg on my face. Why didn't you just go to black?"

Very calmly, he would look at me and say, "Chicago doesn't want us to go to black. Folks don't want to tune in to watch a screen with nothing on it, and so they'll just have to watch you with egg on your face."

Moose was a very big man. Unlike the rest of our crew who dressed in thrift shop clothing, Moose always wore a suit, shirt and tie. He justified his sartorial elegance by being named Channel 2's engineer-in-charge, director and production manager.

The telephone rang again just as I put down the *Rocky*. It was my old friend, Harry Smith, of the Arts and Entertainment television network.

I have known Harry for many years, since he was a disc jockey at KHOW and later worked for Channel 7. CBS then picked him up for duty in Dallas and later with Paula Zahn on its early morning show.

Harry and I have stayed in touch over the years. He called last week to set up a time when he could interview me for the A&E Network. He says he likes to do things like this from time to time with folks he likes.

He's coming to my house at 9 a.m. for the shoot. I don't mind admitting to you that I am a little nervous about that. My pattern is that I usually wake up early to shave, shower and shine. Then I grab a quick breakfast and take my early-morning nap.

Will I be too groggy for Harry? And what about my pain medication? My hospice nurse tells me I am not taking enough Roxicet or Roxanol or morphine sulfate. I keep putting it off, thinking the stuff will cloud my thinking.

Will my mouth be too dry for the interview? The narcotics do that to you. Muffy found some neat stuff on the Internet that helps me. It's called SST (Salix Saliva Stimulating tablet). They are little pills that stimulate the saliva glands, but I am about out of them. I guess I can fall back on Tic-Tacs or Wrigley's Big Red chewing gum.

Oh, yes, Angie just arrived for my Thursday massage. I knew something good would happen today!

April 15

Happiness is Harry Smith and a Krispy Kreme

DREAMS.

Harry Smith and his A&E crew left just over an hour ago, his crew being videographer Mike Kalush and his sound person, Katie Peterson. The latter are Denver folks with whom Harry has worked in the past. Mike even recalled that he and Harry once did a piece about me and the old KVOD when I did the morning show and fed the birds.

I was exhausted when they left and couldn't wait to go upstairs and zone out on my bed. But it wasn't long before I sat bolt upright and wanted to come back downstairs and write in my diary before my thoughts escaped.

Harry and company arrived shortly after 9 a.m. with a huge box of Krispy Kreme doughnuts, which Harry knew I coveted. I noticed right away that Krispy Kreme spelled its product doughnut, not donut, the way the Winchell's folks do. I don't know what my spell-check will think about that.

No matter. I was looking forward to our interview because Harry and I are such old and good friends. Maybe it is because we are so much like each other that we always get along so well.

Harry loves his family, as I do mine. He enjoys cooking, as I do. He has a special love for language, as I do. His affection for music is much the same as mine. We like it all. I don't know that Harry does his own laundry, as I do. Maybe we ought to draw the line there.

Anyhow, we just had a wonderful time laughing together, even crying together. We laughed at how easily I cry over the simplest things, like the grand opening of a supermarket. Of course, he wanted to know how I felt about dying and how I reached the point in what is left of my life that I knew it had to end.

We spoke briefly of my thoughts about a hereafter, if there is one. I tried to describe for him how hospice care has helped me through the last stage of my life. I showed him the array of narcotics I take to help me ward off pain. I spoke of how important Trish and my family are to me, especially my grandson, Jacob.

Mike toted his camera around our house so viewers could see how and where Trish and I live. I was delighted she returned from her shopping trip before we were through.

You don't know Trish, and not many people know her well. And so I was pleasantly surprised when I returned from going upstairs to see that Harry, Mike and Katie had cornered her and Harry was actually interviewing her.

Not in a million years would I have thought she would have stood still for that, but she did. As I listened to her, I was astonished at how forthcoming she was. I couldn't have been more pleased.

I asked Harry to bring me up to speed on what he was doing. On April 19, he is hosting a huge, two-hour A&E special on behind the scenes of *Saturday Night Live.* He said he had a ball doing it. Harry said the process of putting together the show is much the same now as it was in the beginning.

Harry and his wife, Andrea, still live with their kids in an apartment overlooking Central Park in New York. He adores walking through the park every morning he is in town. Somehow, he finds time to be on the board of the Albert G. Oliver Foundation, which helps young black and Hispanic kids fulfill their dreams before they even realize they have dreams.

It was just a great day. I loved every minute of it, especially the Krispy Kremes.

April 17

What's this pain? Just have to wait

SETBACK.

There I was, feeling proud of myself for the neat interview I had with Harry Smith for A&E, when a sharp pain stabbed down from my right hip into my leg. I couldn't stand or walk. It was the first time since I entered hospice that I was completely helpless.

As I was crumpled up on the floor, I tried to figure out what had happened to me. All that pain was on my right side. Until then, the surgery on my left hip had left me with the pain that was my big problem. I didn't know what to do.

My hospice nurse was out of town, and so Trish called the hospice nurse on duty for instructions. She suggested immobilizing the pain area and alternating hot and cold compresses. She also said to continue taking morphine sulfate for general pain and Roxicet for bone pain. There is a difference, and I am never quite sure what it is.

This was a major setback for me. I didn't want to spend the rest of my life in bed, waiting to die. I wanted to remain as active as I could, writing my diary and staying involved with my family and friends. I just hate being dependent on others. I want to be able to take care of myself as much as possible. All this was very depressing.

Still, though, there were some X-ray films of my hip that had not been analyzed, and Dr. Seibert was out of town for the weekend. I needed to talk to her and see her if possible. I didn't have a clue on how I would ever be able to get in a car to go to her office.

I don't know what I would have done without Trish to help me through all of this, even the simplest things. I have to say, she just looks great. Maybe all this running up and down stairs, doing piles of laundry and cooking all these special-diet meals agrees with her.

I wanted to talk to our publisher, John Temple. I didn't know how I would continue to write my diary, or even if the *Rocky* would want me to. John, of course, put my mind at ease about that.

My hospice nurse returned from out of town, examined me and prescribed much of the same therapy recommended by the hospice nurse on duty the day I became hurt, or whatever happened to me.

The problem was, I didn't fall, or strike anything, or do anything that could have caused an injury.

My regular hospice nurse has noticed over the weeks that my gait, or the way I try to walk, is somewhat skewed to the right, trying to lessen the pain on my left hip. She thinks that may be part of the problem, made even worse by the fact that I am an old man with brittle bones that can fracture easily.

If that turns out to be the case, a fracture, I have the option of returning to the hospital for surgery, or maybe just to sweat it out. I don't know yet what I shall do. I'll just have to wait until I know more.

Meanwhile, I scored a major victory today by being able to walk downstairs to write this diary page on my Gateway. Muffy is cleaning up her old laptop in case I need it to avoid taking those painful steps up and down on our stairs. She can lash it up to the phone in my bedroom. She is so good at that kind of thing. Whatever works, I say.

My nurse thinks I should avoid using the stairs whenever possible. That's OK by me.

April 19
Birds make the day even more precious

BIRDS.

Where do I start? Probably with a phone call to Dr. Seibert's office to make an appointment for Thursday. Wednesday is her day off. She must have been there, though, because she called me right back and told me it was OK to come right in and she would see me.

Who says doctors are indifferent? Mine isn't. Anyhow, she had been out of town, and so I went through with her all the aches and pains I had suffered this past week.

She gave me a complete work-up of all my moving parts and decided I ought to have an MRI examination, which I was able to do because there is a radiology facility right down the hall. It wasn't complete but sufficient to rule out some issues.

At the moment, she feels the problem might be spinal, given my past history of back surgery and the twisted conformation of my spinal column. It will take a day or two for the radiology guys to read the films. She said previous films show fairly clear images of both the left and right hips.

So, that's where we go from here. She understands my apprehension of further hospitalization that perhaps would mean lying for hours on a gurney, waiting for a hospital bed to become available.

I realize hospital staffs are doing the best they can with limited resources. I know all that, but I just don't want to be a part of any hospitalization anymore. I admire the overworked nurses and other staffers who are still hanging in there.

I am aware of these problems because they are still calling our house to try to hire my wife, who swears she will never be a hospital nurse again.

Ever.

She means it, too. Other retired RNs will understand her firmness on this issue.

As for me, I am still in big-time pain, but my hospice nurse tells me it is OK to double up on morphine and Roxicet drugs, which I am now doing, even though I wonder if they are clouding my thought process and interfering with whatever writing skills I have left.

I had a nice e-mail from Harry Smith. He wrote to me after returning to New York the night of the interview in our home. No, I don't know when A&E plans to use the interview on its Biography Channel, if that's where it will be scheduled. When I find out, I'll give you a heads-up in my diary.

Mary Ann Nickolay, our next-door neighbor, was sweet enough to bring over some heavenly chicken soup for Trish and me for our dinner tonight.

As rough as it has been bouncing around in Trish's car today and in my wheelchair, it was just great to get out of this house. I have memorized these four walls over and over.

I looked out of the car window, and all of a sudden it was spring. This warm weather—global warming or not—was welcome news for me because so many of the flowering trees and shrubs are beginning to bloom.

The buds on our aspens are popping—and just in time. The birds on that crazy clock Trish bought are chirping their little beaks off. Have you seen those clocks advertised on TV? I never thought we would have one, but we do, and it's giving us the time every hour, on the hour, with authentic bird calls. I love it!

I never thought I would make it this far, and I am grateful for all of it. I just closed my eyes and listened to Diana Krall singing "Let's Face the Music and Dance" on the CD in Trish's car and thought to myself, I am so lucky to still be alive for this glorious spring.

April 20

Dr. Garrett has been a rare friend, indeed

BEGOLE.

I keep wondering why I am so lucky, so fortunate to have friends like Ray Garrett. More accurately, Dr. Ray Garrett, M.D., nephrologist, and the man who has helped guide me through some difficult decisions I have had to make about death and dying.

I'm certain he didn't realize it at the time, but his friendship during a tough period in my life helped me in my struggle with some choices I was facing about my future. He helped smooth the road for me. Not only that, but he has broadened our friendship beyond the medical into areas I never suspected were there.

We both have collected paintings of Denver artist Bill Condit. Ray admired mine on the walls of my home.

Another example: Ray is a wonderful listener. He must be. Otherwise, he wouldn't have known my Grandpa Amole planted elm trees around the old Arapahoe County Courthouse that once stood proudly between 15th and 16th streets, and Court and Tremont places in downtown Denver.

Is there anyone to whom I haven't told this story? Hundreds, maybe even thousands, but it was only Ray Garrett who was kind enough to spend his valuable time doing a computer search for the old building and send the results to me, complete with a photoprint from the Western History Department of the Denver Public Library.

The photo came from the George D. Begole collection. He served as Denver mayor, squeezing in between a couple of Ben Stapleton's terms. After Denver failed to sell the abandoned building, it was razed.

It was a picturesque old domed structure, often mistaken for the Colorado Capitol only a few blocks away. The land on which it was built later became known as Courthouse Square, a lovely little park in downtown Denver.

Unfortunately, we were all seized with a growth-at-any-price mentality, and the little park, along with Grandpa Amole's elms, were peddled to New York developer William Zeckendorf. He replaced it with a Hilton Hotel, which has since undergone several other hotel incarnations.

Anyhow, it was Ray Garrett's kindness that reminded me of the old courthouse and the trees that surrounded it. Our friendship has blossomed into a mutual appreciation of jazz. Otherwise, how would Ray have ever known of my addiction to the piano artistry of Bill Evans, internationally, and Ellyn Rucker locally?

What a really pleasant evening Trish and I spent with Ray at the Burnsley listening to Ellyn, another dear friend of ours! Ray didn't have to, but he was kind enough to send me recordings of Lee Morgan and Stephane Grappelli.

My cup did indeed runneth over when he included CDs of the remarkable Sidney Bechet and *The Ultimate Clifford Brown*.

As soon as I can walk again, we have a standing agreement to visit the Burnsley again for more of Ellyn's magic. I may even wear the Spike Robinson T-shirt she was kind enough to send me from one of Spike's great European concerts.

That's what friends are for!

April 23

This sharp pain just won't leave

BLAH.

This is my first attempt with trying to write a diary page with Muffy's discarded old laptop computer.

Man alive, this is sure slow going. All my fingers have turned into thumbs. My best bet is to return to the old hunt-and-peck system, hammering out my copy with just my forefingers.

It doesn't help that I am just trying to recover from a week of godawful pain that just won't go away. It starts in my right groin and travels up and down my leg to my pelvis and hip, all the way down to my foot and toes. Nothing much seems to help, not even swigs of morphine, which I take regularly.

My problem now seems to be more neurological than it does muscular-skeletal, or something like that. Heck, I don't know. I have about given up trying to understand all these medical terms. Anyhow, I am going in this afternoon for some spinal injections that may help.

Something that has helped me is a little gizmo called a Power Massager. The power comes from two AA batteries. It's tubular in shape and about five inches long and is covered with approximately 200 little sharp metal points. There is an off/on switch at one end.

When I switch it on, the little device vibrates like crazy. I can roll it around on painful areas, and it gives me some temporary relief. It certainly is no cure, but it sure feels good in the middle of the night when those electric-shock pains are keeping me awake.

I know folks will be e-mailing me, wondering about where they can get the little Power Massager, but I don't know. I have forgotten who gave it to me, but someone will let me know.

I am now pretty much confined to my small bedroom on the second floor of our home. My laptop sits on a drawer on a bookcase filled with books I have read. All the Tony Hillermans are there.

Speaking of that, I am concerned about Tony. Is he OK? He has e-mailed me a couple of times, but it seems to me someone told me he isn't well. Over the years I have really enjoyed his Joe Leaphorn and Jim Chee mysteries. I have also learned a great deal about New Mexico's Land of Enchantment and the Navajo culture.

There are just three small high windows in my room permitting me to see the tops of the aspens in our front yard, a large Austrian pine, a pink flowering crabapple tree, and that's about my view of the world.

Jon bought me a Rubbermaid walker at Walgreen's that helps me hobble to the bathroom just outside my door. For now, the stairway is so risky that Trish brings me my meals from the kitchen downstairs. I am still able to take a shower by myself. Thank goodness for that.

What else, now? I have two small statues of soldiers: One is an African-American buffalo soldier before the turn of the last century, and the other is a World War II staff sergeant with a Sixth Armored Division patch on his sleeve. He is carrying a Thompson submachine gun, my weapon of choice during the Big One.

Oh yes, I have cable TV so I can keep track of all our helpless measures to find peace in the Middle East. Sending Colin Powell over there won't do it. All that is just talk. Blah, blah, blah. It all seems too pointless to expect blah, blah to solve hatred that is centuries old.

April 26

Thoughts of sushi start me on a roll

Sushi.

Trish just slipped down to King Soopers for some sushi, which always reminds me of the old Eddie Cantor song, "If You Knew Sushi Like I Know Sushi, Oh, Oh, Oh What A Gal!"

You would have to have been alive back in the 1930s to understand the meaning of that old evergreen and even remember who old Banjo Eyes was. Lordy, how time slips by when you're having fun.

Anyhow, I think of sushi as being "fun food." It's pretty, and I suspect it may even be nutritious. We'll have sushi for dinner tonight, and I may knock back a Tanqueray martini to wash it down.

As he reads this, I can just hear old Ben Blackburn grumbling to Charlene, "Look at this, Geno and Trish are gonna eat raw fish for dinner!"

My first sushi experience was in 1950 when Ichikawa Emiko-san took pity on a lonely American correspondent and accompanied him on a swimming excursion to Kamakura, where the great black Buddha sits impassively for all who pause to contemplate the meaning of life.

But we were not there to contemplate, but to swim and have fun on the volcanic sand beaches and to pack away sushi. Emi-chan's friends made sport of me having my first experience eating raw fish, but I loved it all. No, it didn't taste like chicken.

Chicken tastes like chicken, and don't you forget it! Either crispy fried like Elizabeth Amole fried it, or with dumplings the way Grandma Lizzie Fiedler cooked the old bird when we all came for dinner on Sunday at West 23rd and Newton.

I must be rambling again, but so much of our lives is intertwined with what we eat and drink. Nothing wrong with that, is there? Golly, I hope not.

But getting back to sushi—just got home with our sushi for dinner, and it's about time to eat here. You can tell this is another one of those real-time pieces I write occasionally. I should take care not to splash the soy sauce on the keyboard.

That means I am writing about stuff that is happening to me as I write it, not later, giving me time for reflection. It is probably a good idea I don't write about the martini experience as I am having it, though. I am having enough trouble finding the keys on this little laptop the way it is.

… It's days later now and I am waiting for another spinal injection at Swedish Hospital. They called me a couple of hours ago to firm up my appointment and to reassure me that my epidural injection will make the procedure relatively painless.

In the meantime, my little laptop crashed and I had to have Muffy come over to my cubbyhole and rescue it. Just after she left, I did something that I thought made this diary page MIA (missing in action).

But just as I was about to throw the fool thing out the window, Jon shows up to take my Stingray out for an emission check. Because he is a computer technician, he was able to find my diary page and get me started again.

My kids (middle-age grown-ups) continue to amaze me with their generosity and willingness to take care of their old man. You should have seen Brett the other day, grabbing me by my mutt and pushing me up the stairs.

And Gary and Susan always make my day when they bring Jacob over to delight his grandpa.

Sayonara for this time.

Rocky Mountain News *columnist Gene Amole died at 5:30 p.m. Sunday, May 12, 2002, surrounded by his family in the study where he wrote many of his final columns. This column was written by Gene to be read after his death.*

May 13

Goodbye, Denver

GRUMBLED.

In life, we ask where have I been, and where am I going? In death, I don't know where I am going or if I shall even exist. I have been to a lot of wonderful places, though, and I am grateful for the journey.

Before the fact, I wonder what my last thoughts were. I suspect they were about my family, which is really my measure of immortality. I shall live on through them and through those they beget.

I also would hope that along the way I have said, written or spoken something of value to those who survive me. Certainly, I make no claim of original thought, but perhaps I have taken an existing idea and added some value to it. You are a better judge of that than I.

Eric Satie, the French impressionist composer, wrote a little piano piece titled, "Next-to-Last Thoughts." Since they weren't expressed literally, I have always wondered what they were. Last thoughts are always private. We really don't know how, or if, the mind works at the moment of death. I hope my last thoughts were peaceful.

In one of our last conversations, my friend Dorothy Smith and I agreed that our years, compared to all others, were the best. She is 82 now. Dorothy and I had shared V-E Day together in London when I was on leave from the war front.

Because of that war, we had both seen the world at its worst, and yet we cherished our memories of it because it revealed our people at their best. We both shared our fears of the future, not for us, but for those who are succeeding us.

Somehow, though, the goodness of people always finds a way to come to the surface during times of great peril. It is my hope that this will again be our world's salvation.

It has been difficult for me to leave my Denver. Yes, it is my Denver. I own it in much the same fashion as poet Thomas Hornsby Ferril claimed ownership of City Park where he walked his dog and marveled at sunsets.

Sure, I have grumbled about changes not to my liking, but there is something unique about this place that will always be the Denver where I was born and lived most of my life. I can't describe it precisely. Maybe it has something to do with seeing the mountains every day.

Or maybe it is the prairie that sprawls clear to the horizon, far to the East. Those wind-punctured plains have their beauty, too. To be able to look up at night from them and see the Milky Way splashed across the sky makes the heart pump with pleasure.

Of course, people make the city, or is it that the city makes the people? I don't know, but whatever the reason, Denver people are special. They care for others. They are courteous. They are kind.

I was privileged to spend many of my last years at this proud old newspaper. To work here and become a part of its legacy was a great gift to me.

How fortunate I was to have had my family near me when I died. I lived for them. They were my reason to be. I hope they know how much I really loved them.

Now, I'm gone.

Goodbye.

Recalling Gene Amole

(Editorial from the *Rocky Mountain News*)

There was no one in Colorado journalism as immense as Gene Amole. Only when you understand that will you begin to have an inkling of what his passing means.

There was no one else whose career linked the beginnings of Denver television with later success in both radio and print—and no one, certainly, who was an unexcelled master at each medium.

There was no one else who spoke with such unchallenged authority about Denver before and after World War II; no one whose memory spanned so much of Denver's past who continued to care so much about the city's future, too.

There was no one else who reached so effortlessly across generations to tell important stories about who we are—our hopes and fears, our ugly and better selves—in the simple prose of a folk tale. Gene combined the old-time journalist's gruff and biting attitude toward news with a watchmaker's attention to cadence and a concertmaster's delight in perfect pitch. He could write about anything and the subject simply sprang to life.

Not only was there no one like Gene Amole in Denver, there will never be the likes of him again.

We say this in part because Gene's talent was a starburst rather than a formula waiting to be stolen. And because Gene was a symbol of the city in a way no future journalist can hope to match. The city Gene grew up in was a place that an individual could still get his arms around and understand. Gene sank roots deep and wide, and so everything he said about Denver rang with raw experience and honest conviction.

There will be good and great journalists in the years to come, but they won't mean to Denver what Gene Amole has meant.

Always the professional craftsman, Gene once asked us to warn him if we saw him losing his touch. He figured he'd be the last to know when his skills began to fade or he started to write aimless columns that left readers scratching their heads. He was a man with pride in his work and he didn't want to embarrass himself. Yet of course he never did, as those who read his columns over the past few months already know.

If anything, Gene's columns about his approaching death moved and reached more people than any similar stretch of writing during his entire career.

Like Gene, the rest of us at the *Rocky Mountain News* have pride in our work, too. But we are also realists. If we're honest with ourselves, we know that when we leave this paper there will be 100 other writers or editors or photographers or designers who can step into our shoes, and that one of them most certainly will. Gene was the shining exception, and that is why his memory is so special. We are humbled by his accomplishment, even if we don't quite understand how he did it. We are like those natives on Easter Island who, when asked by explorers how their ancestors managed to build monuments of such astonishing size and haul them from place to place, could only shake their heads in wonder. How does a single journalist connect so personally with so many people for so many years and never lose his touch?

We simply don't know. Only Gene Amole knew the secret—and now, to our great loss, he is no longer here to work its magic.